InterfaceTheology:
Volume 3, Number 1, 2017

Subscription rates
Print: Local: Individual Aus $55, Institutions Aus $65.
Overseas: Individuals US $60, Institutions US $65.

Interface Theology is a biannual refereed journal of theology published in print, epub and open access by ATF Press in Australia.
The journal is a scholarly ecumenical and interdisciplinary publication, aiming to serve the church and its mission, promoting a broad based interpretation of Christian theology within a trinitarian context, encouraging dialogue between Christianity and other faiths, and exploring the interface between faith and culture. It is published in English for an international audience.

ISSN 2203-465X
Cover design by Astrid Sengkey. Text Minion Pro Size 11

978-1-925679-16-8 soft
978-1-925679-17-5 hard
978-1-925679-18-2 epub
978-1-925679-19-9 pdf

An imprint of ATF Theology part of the ATF Press Publishing Group.
ATF (Australia) Ltd.
PO Box 504
Hindmarsh SA 5007
Australia
www.atfpress.com
Making a lasting impact

Congar and Chenu
Friend, Teacher, Brother

InterfaceTheology 3/1 2017

Table of Contents

Interface Theology 3/1 2017

Two brothers: Chenu and Congar

Timothy Radcliffe OP

I entered the front door of the Priory of St Jacques in Paris one late September day in 1973 to begin a year of studies in the Dominican community that was the successor to Le Saulchoir. The brother at the porter's lodge, frère Philippe, phoned the guest master. While I waited an ancient brother shuffled up, gave me an amiable punch, pulled my hair and wandered off. I assumed that it was just a brother who had lost his mind.

Later that evening the community gathered for the lecture to open the academic year. It was to be given by the famous Marie-Dominique Chenu. To my horror, the ancient friar whom I had met that afternoon, meandered up to the lectern. I hoped that some kind soul would steer him away. But no, it was Chenu!

It quickly became clear that in order to pay for my board and lodging, I would have to get a job, since my province was too impoverished to pay the bills. The prior suggested that in partial payment I could be for the year an assistant to the other famous Dominican in the community, Yves Congar. It was not a grand position. I made him tea and coffee, photocopied articles and checked translations from English. But it meant that I met him once or twice every day and we came to have a quiet friendship.

It is perhaps the greatest privilege of my life to have spent a year with these two brothers. In my office at Santa Sabina when I was Master, I had behind my desk, keeping a watch over me, a photograph of them sitting together during recreation after lunch in St Jacques. They are turned towards each other, Congar is animatedly making a point, which Chenu appears to welcome with an open hand. When Gustavo Gutierrez came to talk about joining the Order, he spotted the photo and loved it, and so of course I had to give it to him.

Two men who were so close and who had supported each other during the hard times and rejoiced together at the transformation of the Church at the Council, and yet so different in style. Congar was always a teacher, even when he preached; Chenu was always a preacher, even when he lectured. The community mass was at midday though nearly all of the community was absent at that time. Congar would give one a formal kiss of peace, whereas Chenu would embrace one with a warm hug. But both them, in their different ways, were pre-eminently our brothers. When Yves was asked how he had endured so much he replied, 'le fait des frères enfin'.[1] The fact of the brotherhood. It was, he said, with the brethren that he found happiness. Three years before I met him, Chenu said at a lecture in Toulouse that every time the gospel awoke, the word 'frères' was renewed in its strength and vigour.[2] At a time when Pope Francis is challenging us to move beyond clericalism, the fraternity which these two embodied is a lesson we need to learn now.

Most evenings some of the younger brethren would have a beer around 10pm in the refectory. Although he was nearly 80, Chenu would come back from meetings with academics, artists, trade union leaders, and share his impressions of the day. He would then ask: 'And what you have you learnt today?' He was an eternal student.

Congar was less extroverted but I found him always amiable and even-tempered. I never found him rude or gruff during the year that I was with him. He was immensely generous with his time. Despite the physical suffering that he endured, the pains of his childhood, the attacks of the Holy Office, he had a magnanimity of heart.

One particular occasion stands out when his patience was a little tested. To celebrate his 70th birthday, there was a public seminar. Introducing the discussion of Congar's contribution to the Second Vatican Council, the Regent of Studies, frère Jean-Pierre Joshua OP, praised Congar at length but then said, 'mais maintenant nous sommes ailleurs'. 'Now we are elsewhere!' This was less than nine years after the end of the Council, and yet there was an impression that we had moved beyond those debates. This clearly irritated Congar and he was right. We had hardly begun to enact the Council. I told Yves that in the English Province we would have had a party!

---

1. *Journal d'un théologien : 1946–1956* (Paris: Cerf, 2000), 422.
2. 'L'Ordre de Saint Dominique a-il-encore sa chance?' unpublished lecture given 11th October 1970 at Toulouse.

I often think that I failed to listen attentively enough to what frère Yves had to teach us. We did have a feeling that we had moved on. The arrogance of youth! He would lecture to a full room, with perhaps 80 to a hundred students. Once I accepted an invitation to go to the cinema and skip an evening lecture, thinking that my absence would not be noticed. Alas it was Yves asked where I was and then said that he would wait until I arrived, which I did not. This led to a rebuke from the Regent. I never missed another class.

One day I called to see if there was anything that I could do for him and I found in front of him on his desk a high stack of papers. He told me that it was his diary of the Council. I asked if I could read it and he replied that it was under embargo until anyone who might be hurt by his outspoken commentary on the participants was dead! The first volume was published in 2002.

At the end of the year, to thank me for my assistance, he offered to take me on a visit to Chartres Cathedral. Together with a friend of mine, Michael Oborne who was teaching in Paris, we took frère Yves, together with his wheelchair, in the car and spent the day there. He gave me perhaps the greatest theological lesson of my life.

I do not remember seeing him again until I visited him in *Les Invalides* in the early nineties. He was virtually paralysed but he seemed at peace. He told me that he had only managed to write one short book that year. For me it seemed miraculous that he had written anything at all in such conditions. Shortly afterwards, he was appointed a cardinal. The delicate question was: Who would bestow the red hat? The Secretary of State proposed one candidate. Congar replied that this man was stupid and rejected the suggestion. Another was proposed, and Congar's reaction was typical: 'Il est encore pire! Il est enmerdant!' Finally, it was agreed that Cardinal Johannes Willebrands, Congar's great ally at the Council and in the cause of Christian Unity, should represent the Pope, accompanied by Daniel Cadrin OP, a member of the Order's General Council. The room was filled with young French soldiers who had been wounded in the Balkans, gathered to celebrate this great Frenchman.

He died while I was away from Rome, I think on visitation of the Russian and Ukrainian Vicariate. I was summoned to Notre Dame de Paris to preach. Somehow a sermon was prepared, I suspect with the help of Guido Vergauwen OP, the Socius for Intellectual Life and subsequently Rector of Fribourg University. His funeral was attended by the entire French hierarchy. Arriving from cold, I put my habit on over warm winter clothing, and over that I was robed with an alb and then a chasuble. With so many layers of clothing, I waddled to the lectern to preach, fearing that I would be overcome by the heat.

It was an honour to have spoken at the funeral of this courageous brother, the master teacher, and whose work for the renewal of the Church is still in the process of bearing fruit.

InterfaceTheology 3/1 2017

Yves Congar OP
A Man of the Church, a Man of faith, a Man of the Gospel
My memories

Eric T de Clermont-Tonnerre OP

My meeting with Yves Congar has marked my life as a Dominican religious since the period of my theological studies in Strasbourg, until the last years of the life of this great figure of the Church of the twentieth century and of the Order of the Preachers who, among a few others, had already led me, although young, to be interested in theology and in the Dominicans.

As Prior Provincial of the Dominican Province of France to which Congar, as you know, belonged, I lived by his side as a brother Dominican in his elevation to the cardinalate, and then, in 1995, at his death and his funeral. Then it was with my agreement and my collaboration—somewhat minimal—that we had published through Cerf the *Journal de la Guerre (1914–1918)*, the *Journal d'un théologien (1946–1956)*, and had prepared the edition of *Mon Journal du Concile (tome I, 1960–1963, et tome II, 1964–1966)*, all of which have been translated into English and to which I will refer below.

First meeting

My generation of young Dominican students was the last to take classes with Yves Congar, in 1980 or 1981. It was a course on ecclesiological doctrines. There were about ten students gathered around our somewhat disabled Dominican brother—who was somewhat like a grandfather to us—in his room at the Residence Sertillanges next to the Convent [Priory] Saint-Jacques in Paris. Congar was in a wheelchair and when he needed to read a book or show us something he asked a student brother to grab it for him from one of his shelves pointing with his cane at the book. He grew impatient when the student brother could not find the book at first, as he was also nervous and impatient when he was helped on his travels or up a flight of stairs or into a car: angry if he was helped, angry if we did not help him. Yves Congar, who had to fight from early on in his life with a disease that gradually but surely gnawed at him which led him to be overcome, or a little angry. But he was also a very fraternal man. I was told that at the Convent of Studies at Le Saulchoir or at the Convent of Saint-Jacques, he sometimes slipped a note into the locker of a brother to ask his pardon for having been too carried away. Sometimes this confession was public: he asked all the brothers to excuse him for his bad character.

Congar was also somewhat authoritarian. In Strasbourg, where he was sent after his exile in Jerusalem and Cambridge and where he was still residing at the opening of the Second Vatican Council, to help his mobility he used to like to go to a local swimming pool every week with another brother. To make this time profitable, he bought two subscriptions. And to not lose the tickets, you had to be regular. They would swim in this municipal swimming pool whether there was sun or rain. And it was Congar who led the event. To his companion he would say: 'I hope you have brought something to read!', 'We are going to swim!', 'We can now go and read!', or 'We can go swimming again!' and then 'We can go back to the priory!' . . .

This fiery, combative, authoritarian character came from his family background. Originally from Sedan, a border region close to Germany, the Congars were used to conflict with their hated neighbor. Coming from this region where the forests are populated with numerous and large game, Congar was nicknamed the 'wild boar of the Ardennes'; and he had in his room a frame containing the picture of a wild boar.

Cardinal

It was as Prior Provincial of the Dominican Province of France, from 1992 to 2001, that I renewed my contact with Yves Congar about a decade after I first met him. I went to visit him several times at the *Hôpital des Invalides*, a military hospital where he was admitted because of his years of captivity and where he was very much liked by all the staff. Although he was very sensitive to the staff, he was much less sensitive to the Domincan brothers who came to visit him. The first time I went there I was very afraid that it would be unpleasant as it had been for my predecessor as Provincial, Fr Francis Marneffe, who was reproached for being 'the fifth visitor of the day' which was very tiring! I often wondered why he had been so kind to me when I visited even though I was very intimidated and did not have much to bring him. Reflecting, I wondered if seeing that I was born with a disability with the right hand, there was not some form of delicacy coming from that gruff but tender heart that knew the handicap (his which was much more painful and constraining than mine).

In November 1994, Yves Congar was created a Cardinal by Pope John Paul II. This news upset him so much that his health would deteriorate very quickly after and he died seven months later. The emotion was too great: he who had not stopped working in 'this Church which I love!' He who had been criticised, denounced, suspected, then sanctioned, exiled and who had, after all, 'worked so much' for the Church at the Second Vatican Council, was hurt by this belated recognition of the Church and by the Pope, which made him feel a mixture of joy and pain: joy in the Church and for the Church which he had served; and a very real pain for all that he had gone through in his life. He quickly asked his nephew, Dominique Congar to go to the Parisian district of Saint Sulpice to a shop to buy the red cap and a pectoral cross. Dominique went to the address indicated and bought the pectoral cross for his uncle. As for the red cap, there are several sizes. 'Is it for you?', the saleswoman asked. 'No, it's for my uncle Father Congar who has just been made a cardinal!'. 'What size is his head?' 'You can try it on me! I have the same skull as him. He only has less hair.' From now on, at the Invalides hospital, Cardinal Congar welcomed all those who came to congratulate him with his red cap on his head . . .

The succession of visitors moved him but also exhausted him. The preparations for the celebration during which a Cardinal must deliver him, in the name of the Pope, the cardinal's hat irritated him, so much so that many without being asked came to give advice, to make contacts, in short . . . to complicate things for him. Some brothers said that Cardinal Lustiger, the Archbishop of Paris, was eager to hand over the red hat to Father Congar and that he had gone to Rome for that purpose. As Prior Provincial and with my Provincial Council I thought it would be more meaningful to ask Cardinal Willebrands, the former President of the Pontifical Council for the Promotion of Christian Unity, to do this. Information moves quickly in high places and it was discovered that Cardinal Lustiger had not gone to Rome for this request and, in any case, it was clear that only a cardinal of the Roman Curia can be mandated by the pope for the delivery of the red hat to a new Cardinal.

So it was that on December 8, 1994, on the feast of the Immaculate Conception, in the Saint Louis Cathedral of the Invalides, that Father Congar, theologian of the Order of Saint Dominic, a resident of the *Hôpital des Invalides*, received the Cardinal red hat from the hands of Cardinal Willebrands, who said to him: 'This gesture of the Pope expresses the personal joy of the Holy Father and of the whole Church for one of the great theologians of the Second Vatican Council [. . .] Your theology is recognized not only in its breadth and depth, but as one on which one could build the idea of an ecumenical council.'

The future Cardinal was not well. He was in a wheelchair. He was wearing his Dominican habit of the Order of Preachers and a stole. Behind him there were two oxygen tanks, and two doctors in white coats, if needed. I was beside him in my chasuble. The future cardinal had to take an oath. Each proposition that was read out needed the answer 'I believe'. Yves Congar was an eternal believer. He firmly believed in the faith of the Church. That day, in the humility of his illness, he could not say a word. The strength was not there. He heard everything and he responded forcefully, but not by uttering an understandable 'I believe'. It was rather a kind of grunt but very sure, very firm. At his side, at each affirmation, I translated what he could not pronounce, but what he meant in front of everyone and said with all his strength in trying also to make a forceful 'I believe'. The red hat was given to him. Immediately after communion, it was at full speed that doctors took an exhausted Cardinal Yves Congar back to his room.

The funeral

On June 26, 1995, the Notre Dame Cathedral is crowded for Cardinal Congar's funeral.

At the end of the celebration, more than one hundred and fifty Dominican friars come to sing, near the coffin, the antiphon dear to Thomas Aquinas: '*Media vita, in morte sumus . . .*'; 'In the midst of life, we are in death, to whom would we ask for help but to you, Lord?'

The military governor of the Hôpital des Invalides then approached the coffin and addressed the deceased friar in these terms: 'Sir Cardinal, my captain . . .' And under the vaults of the Cathedral resounded the 'Last Post' to the dead. Tribute of the Church, tribute of the Republic, tribute to the fighter!

As for the delivery of Cardinal's casket, a certain Dominican friar from our Province tried to influence matters. While I was in bed with the flu, the said religious, without asking, went to see the Apostolic Nuncio to tell him that the ceremony should take place at the Cathedral Saint Louis des Invalides, where Cardinal Congar had received the red hat. The motivation for his idea was for two reasons: Cardinal Lustiger would certainly not want a celebration at the Cathedral of Notre Dame; and Congar was very old so there would not be many people attending.

When I heard this, I was annoyed, and I got out of bed and phoned Cardinal Lustiger. We were on the same wavelength: this was the Cathedral where the funeral of Cardinal Congar was to be celebrated, in this Cathedral where, during the last twenty years, the Dominicans of the Province of France also celebrated the funeral of Marie-Dominique Chenu, of Ambroise-Marie Carré, as well as a solemn mass in memory of Pierre Claverie, Bishop of Oran, after his assassination.

Le Journal de la Guerre (1914–1918) ou journal d'enfant = Journal of the War (1914–1918) or Child's Diary

Very soon after the death of Congar, there was talk of publishing Le Journal de la Guerre (1914–1918), which the young Yves (ten years) had himself entitled (and writes with his hand on the first of five school notebooks covering the period July 1914–January 1915) Journal de la guerre Franco-Boche 1914–1915 par Yves Congar, illustré de 42 gravures et 2 cartes, de la déclaration 4 août et même du 27 juillet au 25 janvier 1915 [Journal of the Franco-Boche War 1914–1915, illustrated with forty-two engravings and two cards, the declaration 4 August and even from 27 July to 25 January 1915]. At ten years of age, Congar already had the sense of publishing. He wrote his journal and illustrated it as a true author thinking of its publication. Some brothers of our Province were opposed to this publication. But this book honors its author. These notebooks reveal a great gift of observation and show a style so very personal and assertive. And already he showed his desire to note carefully what he observed, what he felt and what he thought.

Here is an excerpt from the first notebook: On August 23, 1914

> . . . the Belgian emigration begins . . . It is hard to see these
> poor Belgians go by, some trailing a child in a pram followed
> by old people walking with difficulty and finally the children
> carrying a light pack in their hand and driving their flocks
> ahead of them, while others with two mattresses on 2 carts
> with crying children on top of them, old men and women
> wailing sadly at their meager possessions.

The inventiveness of the young Yves is astonishing: these poems written in memory of his dog Kiki, poor martyr of the fatherland that the Congars had put down rather than pay the taxes imposed by the Germans; and the quality of his drawings representing Father Toussaint who had not given over his bicycle and was 'stopped by the Boche command' and allowed to leave. We see the priest on his bike with the caption Left!! And in the police station reading his breviary, with the caption Reading the Breviary.

Le Journal d'un théologien (1946–1956) = Journal of a Theologian (1946–1956)

Three years after Editions du Cerf published the *Journal d'un théologien* which gathers several articles and documents concerning the darkest period of our Dominican, the years 1946 to 1956. Barely out of captivity during the Second World War, Congar is exposed to the suspicions and sanctions of the ecclesial authority because of some of his publications: prohibition of teaching, exile . . . Journals of this testing time, these documents constitute an exceptional testimony on the relations between the theological research and the Roman magisterium at the end of the pontificate of Pius XII.

Curiously this book did not meet any major opposition as to its publication. Like the *Journal de la Guerre* and *Mon Journal du Conseil*, it has been a real editorial success in France.

Most poignant in this context is his letter to his mother, dated Cambridge September 10, 1956, for her 80th birthday. I quote some extracts:

> French Dominicans were persecuted and silenced—it is also
> a Church of Silence, in its own way–because they were the
> only ones to have a certain freedom of thought, enterprise and

expression. Admittedly, it was only a freedom in orthodoxy, but an orthodoxy whose sources are also the Bible, the Fathers, etc. The first reproach that was made to me, the only clear one perhaps, was in 1938 or 39; Father Gillet then told me: You are reproached for advocating the return (or recourse) to the sources. And, of course, there are others that we live and work in this direction. Oh yes! There are many, and perhaps more and more. But we know that it is largely thanks to us (the role of Editions du Cerf, etc.). And above all, we are the only ones *as a body* to be free in and for the service of the truth; the only ones, as a body, to put the truth above all.

Practically, they destroyed me. As much as he can be in them, they have destroyed me. Everything I believed in and given to me was taken away:

Ecumenism (I have done nothing, or almost, since 39!)
education
conferences
action alongside priests
collaboration with *Christian Testimony*, etc.; participation in major conferences (Catholic Intellectuals, etc.)

My body was not touched; in principle, one has not touched my soul; I was not asked for anything. But a man's person is not limited to his skin and his soul. Especially when this man is a doctrinal apostle, he *is* his action, he *is* his friendships, his relations, he *is* his normal radiance. They took all that away; we trampled all this, and so I was deeply hurt. I was reduced to nothing and, for all that, they destroyed me. When, at certain moments, I see what I had aspired to be and to do, what I had begun to do, I am seized by an immense heartbreak.

And I know it's without remedy. I know them. I know that when they chase someone, it is until death. Father Sertillanges was allowed to return to France when he was 80 years old. After that, we sometimes say or let others say good things. The Jews also built tombs for the prophets, after killing them. I know that—whatever number of years I still have ahead, 25, 30 years—I will never find freedom of action, nor normal living conditions. All that I have undertaken, all the preparations of my notes, more abundant than what I have been able to get out of here, all this is without issue and without future.

It's atrocious to be killed alive.

Father Congar wanted the diary he kept at the Second Vatican Council to be published. But he had banned publication before the year 2000. With my support, Editions du Cerf embarked on the adventure. But it was a real 'obstacle course'. All wanted to interfere, either to suggest censoring certain passages where Yves Congar was severe in his judgments, or believed in his expressions, or to direct the edition. It took a lot of recourse by Brother Nicolas-Jean Séd, then President of the Executive Board of Editions du Cerf, supported by Dominique Congar, by Brother André Duval, Archivist of the Province of France, and by me to carry out the edition of this journal in a relatively short time.

The book was published when I had completed my mandate as Provincial Prior and joined Editions Cerf!

In 2012 we congratulated ATF Press for initiating the translation of these 1,130 pages as well as the translators and editors who contributed due to the fact that no major English or American publisher wanted to undertake the project till then. After this ATF Press has published the other two books and has further Congar publications in preparation. This is a very big achievement.

May the English-speaking readership learn and enjoy reading these books.

Translated by Helen Frank

Congar and Chenu: Inside and Outside Vatican II

Janette Gray RSM

Among the many treasures in these translated Vatican II diaries of Yves Congar is the detailed intensity of his response to the events of the Council and its working groups and his naming even the least known participants and advisers. One of these is his colleague Marie-Dominique Chenu. Chenu is less acknowledged in the English-speaking world and yet Congar repeatedly wrote of his huge impact on the beginnings of his career and Chenu's continuing presence throughout these momentous events. Together they make an interesting study of the layers of engagement of theological advisers in the Council process, from the direct participation of the *periti* like Rahner, Congar and Ratzinger in commissions and writing parties of the schemas of the Council documents to the more peripheral articulation and agitation of non-official theologians, like Chenu. Congar's diaries indicate more substantially the extensive degree of his involvement in the production and refinement of many of the key Council documents. He was on the inside. Chenu, in contrast, left a much smaller diary record of the Council as yet not translated from the French, which includes more personal detail than Congar claimed to allow himself.[1] As well Chenu had less to recount as he was definitely on the outside of the commissions while very active around the Council giving commentary on and criticism of the documents or on their salient themes.

There is a back story to these co-contributors to Vatican II that deserves some elaboration in order to appreciate the depth of their

---

1. Marie-Dominique Chenu OP, *Notes quotidiennes au Concile: Journal de Vatican II 1962–1963*, ed. by Alberto Melloni (Paris: Éditions du Cerf, 1995).

collaboration. There is no doubt that Congar is the greater theologian but for energy and engagement with the world even Congar was in awe of Chenu's contribution. The story begins with Chenu teaching Congar at the old *Le Saulchoir* in Belgium from 1926–30.[2] There he taught the history of Christian doctrines emphasising the historical vicissitudes of doctrine which dictated the direction of his future theology.[3] As Congar later commented:

> It was the history of doctrine where he exposed us to finding the truth of history, that is the drama where one takes the part of each side of a problem and poses what its understanding and misunderstandings involve. . . . One then lived the issues as a problem-solving exercise.[4]

Congar also recalled that it was Chenu's influence that encouraged him into the theology of ecumenism. Later when they were colleagues at *Le Saulchoir*, Congar having joined the faculty in 1931, they conspired to undertake the elimination of the official theological 'system' of 'modern-scholasticism', which they derogatively termed 'baroque', for its atemporal, over-analytical and static metaphysical approach:

> One day, chatting at the entrance of the old Saulchoir, we found ourselves in profound accord - at once intellectual, vital and apostolic - on the idea of undertaking a 'liquidation of baroque theology'. This was a moment of intense and total spiritual union. We elaborated a plan and distributed the tasks among ourselves. I still have the dossier that was begun then. . . .
>
> It was not a question of producing something negative: the rejections were only the reverse of aspects that were more positive. . . . What would a little later be called 'ressourcement' was then at the heart of our efforts.[5]

While Congar claimed this was not 'revolutionary', he and Chenu were soon censured and Chenu was removed from his post as Regent

---

2. Yves Congar 'The Brother I have Known' *Thomist* 49 (1985): 495–503.
3. M.-D. Chenu and Jacques Duquesne, *Un théologien en liberté: Jacques Duquesne interroge le Père Chenu* (Paris: Le Centurion, 1975), 48.
4. Congar, 'The Brother I have Known', *The Thomist*, 49 (1985), 495–503 (495).
5. Congar, 'The Brother I have Known', 499.

of Studies at *Le Saulchoir* by the Master General of the Dominicans Gillet 'for recommending a return to the sources', which was deemed the Modernist heresy. Congar later made a crucial distinction that this was not a 'mere detached, scholarly reconstruction nor a futile attempt at [what he calls] "repristination".'[6] Their conspiracy had immediate if not the desired effect. On publishing its manifesto *Une école de théologie: le Saulchoir*, Chenu was condemned by Mgr Pietro Parente, later Archbishop of Perugia and of the Holy Office, for discrediting Thomism and dishonouring Aquinas because Chenu advocated an historical approach to Thomas and that philosophy studies should involve engagement with philosophy since the Enlightenment.[7] Early in Congar's *Journal of the Council*, Parente is labelled 'the fascist, the monophysite'.[8] This combination of political and theological invective is common to Congar's and Chenu's estimation of their opponents in the Church. They understood such deficiencies as both influenced by, and a collusion with the prevailing political forces of the time [*Action Française*] as much as by their insufficient commitment to the Incarnation and its implications. This is particularly a recurring motif in Chenu's writings. Later, following the controversy about the worker-priests and the replacement of the three French Dominican Provincials by the Master-General, Congar and Chenu also were exiled from Paris,[9] Congar to Jerusalem, Cambridge, where he lived next door to Michael Ramsay, yet to become the Anglican Archbishop of Canterbury, and finally to Strasbourg. Chenu was sent to Rouen, and eventually allowed back to Paris one week each month to teach at the École des Hautes Études..[10]

Given these events, for Congar and Chenu, the accession of Pope John XXIII in 1959 held little hope of changing the attitude of the Church by which they had been repeatedly condemned under his predecessor, Pope Pius XII. To the wider Catholic world Guiseppe Roncalli was an unknown Vatican diplomat. To these French Domin-

---

6. Congar, *Vrai et fausse réforme dans l'église* (Paris: Cerf, 1950), 337.
7. Père Parente (1942): 'ce discrédit retombe sur saint Thomas.' cited by Chenu in his preface to 'La théologie comme science au XIIIe siècle' (1943).
8. Yves Congar OP, *My Journal of the Council* (Adelaide: ATF, 2012), 6.
9. Thomas O'Meara OP, 'Raid on the Dominicans':The Repression of 1954', *America*, 2/5/94, 170/4:
10. Fergus Kerr OP, 'Yves Congar' in *Twentieth Century Catholic Theologians* (Oxford: Blackwell, 2007),36.

icans he had been the Vatican's nuncio in Paris immediately before the condemnation of the worker-priests. His role, whether complicit in this condemnation or merely passive, remains undisclosed.[11] When as Pope, he called the Second Vatican Council (1959) their curiosity was raised. Congar was appointed by the Pope among the 200 'experts' to assist in the ante-preparatory stage of the Council.[12] The Curia monopolised the processes that created the disappointing preparatory schemas for the Council and they continued to withhold detailed information from these 'experts'. There was also confusion resulting from the Pope's contradictory decrees. Chenu commented to Karl Rahner: 'The Council has become an operation of the intellectual police within the closed walls of the [neo-scholastic] School.' Chenu further concluded that this evidenced "A sad, belligerent meanness of spirit."[13] on the part of the Curial officials.

In contrast to Congar, Chenu's involvement in the Council was peripheral. He was only there as the personal theologian of his former student, the francophone Madagascan Bishop, Claude Rolland.[14] Chenu spent most of the sessions outside St Peter's. He also consulted with and advised the Eastern-rite bishops, third-world bishops and theologians, other recently suspect theologians, while giving strategic inputs on schema topics to many interested bishops.[15] Congar wryly

---

11. Étienne Fouilloux, 'The Antepreparatory Phase, the Slow Emergence from Inertia (January, 1959 — October, 1962)' in Giuseppe Alberigo and Joseph A. Komonchak (eds.), *History of Vatican II. Volume I*, (Maryknoll/Leuven: Orbis/Peeters, 1995), pp. 54–156, (p. 90). Peter Hebblethwaite's biography failed to unearth Roncalli's attitude to the worker-priests or to the general condemnation of 'nouvelle théologie' in *Humani generis*, except that 'Roncalli was not directly involved in the purge'. *John XXIII. The Pope of the Council*, (London, DLT, 1984), pp. 227–230.

12. Kerr, 43–44.

13. Chenu, Letter to Karl Rahner 4 septembre 1962, Archives de Saulchoir, Paris, Fonds Chenu, *Concile Vatican II*. cited in Chenu, *Notes quotidiennes au Concile: Journal de Vatican II 1962–1963*, ed. Alberto Melloni (Paris: Les Éditions du Cerf, 1995), p.57, n.1.

14. Chenu, *Notes quotidiennes au Concile*, p. 65, n. 2.

15. Chenu's diary recorded meetings with, naturally, Congar and Schillebeeckx, also the French Jesuits Lubac, Daniélou, Rondet, Lyonnet, the Belgian sociologist Houtart, and the Germans Rahner, Grillmeier, and Häring. Alberto Melloni notes that Chenu did not mix with the more powerful theologians of the Council, that he ignored Ratzinger and made little contact with Küng, and Philips. 'Introduction: Les journaux privés dans l'histoire de Vatican II', *Notes quotidiennes au Concile*, pp. 7–54, (p. 50).

observed Chenu's peripatetic activity in his early diary entry: 'In the afternoon, a good visit from Fr Chenu, who sees a great many people: journalists, African bishops, etc.'[16]

Given there is so much material to read in Congar's journal, I have chosen three foci for this talk: each theologian's response to the Opening Ceremony of the Council; the opening communication, *The Message of the Bishops to the World*; their Conciliar contributions.

Opening Ceremony

It is interesting to compare the two theologians' respective responses to the Opening Ceremony of the Council. For Congar it was little short of an abomination. He opens with the setting, St Peter's Basilica:

> I tried to absorb the *genius* loci [spirit of the place] . . . Solemnity, but with a rather cold air about it all. A decorative scheme inspired, as it were, by the theatre of the Baroque. Between the tribunes, the huge statues of the founders of Orders, in their niches. . . . I wish theses statues could speak! What would they say? I imagine what they might say as men of God, consumed by the fire of the Gospel!

Then his criticism moves to the liturgy which contrasted deeply with the 'dialogue Masses' already operative in France:

> The liturgical movement has not yet reached the Roman Curia. This immense assembly says nothing, sings nothing. . . . no liturgy of the Word. I know that in a few minutes a Bible will be placed on a throne in order to preside over the Council. BUT WILL IT SPEAK? Will it be listened to? Will there be a moment for the Word of God?. . . . The whole Church was there, embodied in its pastors. But I regret that a style of celebration was employed that was so alien to the reality of things. What would it have been if those 2,500 voices had sung together at least the *Credo*, if not all the chants of the Mass, instead of that elegant crooning by paid professionals.

---

16. Congar, *My Journal* (18 October 1962); much later he recalled: 'le P. Chenu voyait beaucoup de monde; il allait tous les jours à la salle de presse. Il commentait les texte et les événements, de sorte qu'il a ainsi contribué à une formation de l'opinion. Congar, 'Hommage au Père M.-D. Chenu', *Revue des sciences philosophiques et théologiques*, 75.3 (1991), 361–2, p. 362.

Congar resolved from this event:

> I returned with an immensely stronger desire: 1) to be evangelical, to aim at being a *homo plene evangelicus* [human being fully dedicated to the Gospel]; 2) to WORK. THAT produces results. THAT remains. That will prepare for the next Council, a state of things where what is missing today will be taken for granted.[17]

What insight and prescience these comments show about the key moves for reform that eventuated in THIS Council not the 'next': liturgical reform that engaged not only the bishops but all the People of God in responsive engagement in the Mass and celebration of the sacraments, the Biblical renewal that released the Word of God throughout the Catholic community, and a Council that addressed 'the reality of things'. He further commented more positively: "I see how Eastern the Church is.' Then more negatively: 'To emerge from the Constantinian era has never been part of its programme'. Congar blamed Pius IX for such an imperial misunderstanding of *ekklesia* Congar : 'he oriented the Church to be always OF the world and not yet FOR the world'.[18] Here he made a crucial point about the next great theme of the Council-to-come, the Church in the world, again anticipating the struggles around Schema XIII, *Gaudium et spes*. This consciousness of the world as the theological locus of the Gospel, the place of the Incarnation, is a recurring focus of his ecclesiology.

In some contrast Chenu did not penetrate the sanctuary of St Peter's but attended the end of the ceremony outside with the crowd in St Peter's Square. He was sitting at the base of one of Bernini's columns, where he observed: 'It was very impressive. The Roman grandeur. But also the simple solemnity of this long file of 2,300 bishops in great white copes, topped with mitres.' But his focus drifted to the kindness of a young Italian woman who thought he had collapsed from the heat and gave him a handkerchief impregnated with eau de cologne to revive him. He concluded:

> What a tasteful gesture of this very pretty Italian woman. There was nothing to see of the Council; but I appreciated so

---

17. Congar, *My Journal*, (11 October 1962), 86–7.
18. Congar, 88.

much this generous response of the ordinary person in the midst of this solemnity.[19]

Again the later themes of the Council are anticipated, this time the role of the laity in the Church, a common commitment of both Congar and Chenu in the decades before the Council. Like Congar, Chenu was also concerned that the Council reflect a turn to humanity, not only as a theoretical principle but as a reality, located in history and the world. Despite Chenu's theological sympathy with the announcement of a conciliar *aggiornamento*, for Chenu the Council's world consciousness entailed a more signifiicant perspective. He discerned this in the pre-Council call to the local bishops to register their *vota* or desires for the forthcoming Council. This presented the reluctant Curia with an unprecedented poll of the issues facing the Catholic world (over 2,000 documents), which allowed the local bishops across the world to overthrow the narrow agenda of the Curia.[20] No longer could papal rule alone define the Church's authority, instead a 'Catholicity' that was signified by dialogue and collegiality was needed.[21] For Congar this consultation itself marked a new way of doing ecclesiology, as dialogue with the 'realities' of the local Church, through its universal reach. As Chenu was to reflect later, *aggiornamento* signalled for him 'the entry of the Church day by day in the advance of the world and of history.'[22]

This Thomist openness to the world based on the doctrinal conviction that God continues to work through creation, including humanity, becomes a marker of the two evident trajectories of the Council's theological reformers, the other being a more Augustinian approach. This 'fault line' has become a significant interpretive tool in understanding both the conflicts during the Council and since, as

---

19. Duquesne, *Un théologien en liberté*, 176–7
20. 'Vie conciliaire de l'Église', p. 376. See É. Fouilloux, 'The Antepreparatory Phase: the Slow Emergence from Inertia (January, 1959-October, 1962)' in *History of Vatican II. Volume I*, pp. 55–153, (pp. 97–126) and Thomas F. Stransky SJ, 'The Foundation of the Secretariat for Promoting Christian Unity', in Alberic Stacpole OSB (ed.), *Vatican II by those who were there* (London: Geoffrey Chapman, 1986), 62–87.
21. 'Vie conciliaire de l'Église', 375–6.
22. *Un théologien en liberté: Jacques Duquesne interroge le Père Chenu*, 174.

outlined in significant articles by Gérard Phillips, Joseph Komonchak and David Tracy.[23]

The Bishops' 'Message to the World'

'The Message to the World' from the Bishops of the Council was Chenu's initiative and a most significant intervention in the Council.[24]

> It came to me, in this spirit [of expectation], that an opening declaration by the Council [was needed], a "message" to all people, Christian or not, announcing the aims and inspiration of the Assembly, from a mission perspective and in the context of the problems of the world at this particular time.[25]

Conceived with Congar to counter the inwardness of the prepared Council schemas, Chenu composed a text that amplified the themes of Pope John XXIII's recent allocutions. Chenu had summarised favourably these main themes in 'A Pontificate enters into history' (1963),[26] but he showed some caution about the excessive epithet 'genius' for John XXIII, preferring instead to speak of his 'instinct'. Presumably Chenu recognised in John XXIII 'the instincts of an historian' as noted by Joseph Komonchak in his 'The Struggle for the Council during the Preparation of Vatican II (1960–1962)' in volume 1 of the *History of Vatican II*.[27]

---

23. Gérard Phillips, 'Deux Tendances dans la théologie contemporaine', *Nouvelle Revue Théologique* 85 (1963), 225–238. Joseph A. Komonchak, 'Augustine, Aquinas, or the Gospel *sine glossa?*' in Austin Invereigh (ed.), *Unfinished Journey: The Church 40 Years after Vatican II: Essays for John Wilkins* (NY: Continuum, 2005). 102–118; David Tracy, 'The Uneasy Alliance Reconceived: Catholic Theological Method, Modernity, and Postmodernity', *Theological Studies*, 50 (1989), 548–70.
24. Chenu, 'Le Message au Monde des Pères Conciliaires (20 octobre 1962)', in Yves M.-J. Congar OP, and M. Peuchmard OP (eds.), *L'Église dans le monde de ce temps — réflexions et perspectives*, Unam Sanctam 65c: tome III, (Paris: Cerf, 1967), 191–193.
25. *10–25 September* 1962,. Chenu, *Notes quotidiennes au Concile: Journal de Vatican II 1962–1963* (Paris: Les Éditions du Cerf, 1995), p. 60. [my translation]
26. Chenu,'Un Pontificat entre dans l'histoire' (1963) in *La Parole de Dieu II: L'Évangile dans le temps*, (Paris: Cerf, 1964), 189–198, (192).
27. Joseph A. Komonchak, 'The Struggle for the Council during the Preparation of Vatican II (1960–1962)' in *History of Vatican II. Volume I*, 167–366 (167).

Unusually the *Message* addressed *all* the people of the world, Catholics, other believers, unbelievers. It was this emphasis on communicating beyond the Catholic world that made Chenu's original text deliberately not 'doctrinal' in the apologetic sense, so that even Congar found it too sociological.

> It seemed to me there and then that this initiative was INSPIRED, that it was THIS that was NEEDED! Though I did find Fr Chenu's text a little sociological, too human. Of course it is a message addressed to humankind. But I would have liked there to have been a stronger reference to the fact of Jesus Christ and the offer of the Covenant. Also, I wanted to support Fr Chenu's initiative effectively.[28]

And he did, securing the interest and support of Cardinals Liénart, Alfrink, König, Döpfner, Montini, Frings and Suenens and other Archbishops including Hurley of Durban (SA) and the Coptic bishop of Thebes, Ghattas. He also edited Chenu's text to reflect its themes in 'more ecclesiastical, more biblical' terms.[29] Chenu complained that his 'kid' was doused in holy water.[30] The idea was proposed to the assembly of Bishops and it was accepted on 20 October 1962, with 'no more than twenty' not voting for it.[31]

> We take great pleasure in sending to all men and nations a message concerning that well-being [*salutis*], love and peace which were brought into the world by Christ Jesus, the Son of the living God, and entrusted to the Church.
>
> In this assembly, under the guidance of the Holy Spirit, we wish to inquire how we ought to renew ourselves, so that we may be found increasingly faithful to the gospel of Christ. We shall take pains so to present to the men of this age God's truth in its integrity and purity that they may understand it and gladly assent to it.
>
> Coming together in unity from every nation under the sun, we carry in our hearts the hardships, the bodily and mental

28. Congar, *My Journal*, (16 or 17 September 1962), 81.
29. Congar, (20 October 1962), 101.
30. Chenu
31. Congar, (20 October 1962), 106.

distress, the sorrows, longings, and hopes of all the peoples entrusted to us. We urgently turn our thoughts to all the anxieties by which modern people are afflicted. Hence, let our concern swiftly focus first of all on those who are especially lowly, poor, and weak.

Like Christ, we would have pity on the multitude weighed down with hunger, misery, and lack of knowledge. We want to fix a steady gaze on those who still lack the opportune help to achieve a way of life worthy of human beings.[32]

Chenu judged that while it had a lasting effect on the Council's direction, 'The Message' hardly touched the wider world due to its final clerical tone. As Chenu exclaimed in his 'The Conciliar Life of the Church': 'For God speaks *today*; and that may happen only if his Church is present to the world.'[33] Yet its citation by Pope Paul VI in his opening address of the second session legitimated the concept of *dialogue* with the world, one of the key concepts of the Council, and its themes anticipate many of those of the final Pastoral Constitution of the Council, *Gaudium et spes*.[34] 'The Message to the World' brought to the ecclesial foreground Chenu's and Congar's preoccupation with the Church's relationship with the world, and more specifically a commitment to the world as the locus of the Gospel. It asserted the presence of the Gospel in the world and argued that human values and efforts for peace, promotion of the poor, justice and community, participate in the proclamation of the Gospel like 'toothing-stones' — a metaphor employed by Chenu to evoke building features that protrude in anticipation of future construction or for the completion of a building: 'these supreme human goods are like 'toothing-stones' for the construction of the Kingdom of God.'[35] Congar and Chenu recognised in the world

---

32. 'Message Humanity' in Walter M. Abbott (ed.), *The Documents of Vatican II* (London, Dublin: Geoffrey Chapman, 1966), pp. 3–7. Surprisingly this document does not appear in more recent collections of the Vatican II Documents.
33. 'Vie conciliaire de l'Église', 383.
34. *Un théologien en liberté*, pp. 177–9.
35. Chenu, 'Le message du Concile au monde', in *La Parole de Dieu. II. La Foi dans intelligence*, (Paris: Cerf, 1964), pp. 639–645, (p. 644). Chenu's concept of 'toothing stones' was described further in 'Les Communautés naturelles, pierres d'attente de cellules d'Église (1964)' in *Peuple de Dieu dans le monde* (Paris: Les Éditions du Cerf, 1966), 129–43

both the 'hope and anguish' of human struggle, but not merely as a pastoral strategy for the Church. They aimed to trace the reality of the Incarnation, the humanising of the world, by drawing out the Gospel already there, waiting to be activated through the valuing of human good. The message of 'The Message' was: not that the Church decides that the modern self-confident, autonomous world can be baptised or is ready to be baptised, but that the Church must be there within this world to be near enough to respond *when* the world wants or seeks to be baptised.[36] For Congar and Chenu this was a real world they sought to engage with — so it's not surprising that Congar's journal reports on the two crucial 'outside' events during the Council — the Cuban Crisis and John Kennedy's assassination.

Conciliar Contributions

Congar's extensive contribution to the formulation and revision of many of the Council's documents is systematically tabled in the Journal's excellent appendix 'Chronological Tables Recapitualting Congar's Participation in the Composition of the Various Conciliar Schemas' in the English translation of *My Journal of the Council*, pp. 919–928. Throughout the diary he reports how he is over-committed, especially in the last two sessions and the intersessions dealing with the work on so many of the documents, especially on what became

> *Lumen Gentium* (The Constitution on the Church),
> *Dei Verbum* (On Revelation),
> *Unitatis Redingerato* (Decree on Ecumenism),
> *Sacrosanctum Concilium* (Constitution on the Liturgy),
> *Dignitatis Humanae* (Declaration on Religious Freedom),
> *Presbyterorum Ordinis* (Decree on Priests),
> *Ad Gentes* (Decree on Missionary activity),
> *Nostra Aetate* (Decree on non-Christian Religions),
> *Gaudium et spes* (The Pastoral Constitution of the Church in the World).

Surprisingly despite his pioneering theology on the laity, he was not invited to work on the commission for *Apostolicam actuositatem*,

---

36. Chenu, 'Une Constitution Pastorale de l'Église' (1965) in *Peuple de Dieu dans le monde*, (Paris: Cerf, 1966),. 11–33.

the Decree on the Laity. Congar responded so generously even in ill-health to these substantial commitments. Today I want to focus on Congar's long journey from 1963 through the Council of Schema XVII which became Schema XIII, and eventually was promulgated on 7 December 1965 as *Gaudium et Spes* (The Pastoral Constitution of the Church in the World). As Éric Mahieu comments in the detailed introduction to this translation of the *Journal*, Congar made a determined commitment to 'defending the existence of the schema'.[37] Congar himself declared: 'There was some gigantism in the undertaking of schema XIII.' Largely because of the many layers of contributions, rewriting and the contested ground on key anthropological issues.[38] Congar continued often daunted by the many revisions and drafts of this history-changing document.

In a note recognising Chenu's hidden role in the themes taken up in Schema XIII, Roberto Tucci SJ, who was a member of the sub-commission on culture, observed that Chenu's talk 'A Pastoral Constitution of the Church', where he defended the appropriateness of the name and sense of the document as pastoral, had important repercussions for its acceptance by the Bishops in the second debate in 1965.[39] This too was the focus of Congar's interventions as he wrote later: 'The pastoral is no less doctrinal, but it is doctrinal in a way that is not content with conceptualising, defining, deducing and anathematising: it seeks to express the saving truth in a way that reaches out to the men and women of today, takes up their difficulties, replies to their questions.'[40] Similarly, earlier in the Council (20 November

---

37. Congar, *My Journal*, xix.
38. Congar, (13 September 1965), 773
39. He identifies Chenu's contribution further: 'Notons en passant que cette intervention, comme tant autres précédentes du même auteur, sont d'autant plus appréciables, si l'on considère que, à la surprise générale, il n'avait pas été désigné parmi les experts du Concile et pas même parmi les experts officiels de la Commission mixte, quoique indirectement par ses écrits et ses consultations privées, il eût exercé une influence notable sur la rédaction du Schéma XIII'. Roberto Tucci SJ, 'Introduction historique et doctrinale: Ferments rénovateurs durant la Troisième Session Conciliaire (14 septembre — 21 novembre 1964)' in Yves M.-J. Congar OP and M. Peuchmard OP (eds.), *L'Église dans le monde de ce temps — réflexions et perspectives* (*Unam Sanctam* 65 b tome II), (Paris: Cerf, 1967), pp. 73–127, (p.102, n.97).
40. Congar, 'Théologie *historique*' in *Le Concile de Vatican II. Son Églisepeuple de Dieu et corps du Christ* (Paris, Beauchesne: 1964), 64.

1962) Congar expressed concern about the tension between the Central Theological Commission and the Secretariat for Unity on the earliest schema *De Ecclesia*:

> because it is concerned with PRINCIPLES, whereas the Secretariat is concerned with PRACTICAL questions.
>
> Always this false distinction between categories which I perceived from the very first day as THE most decisive vice of the institution.[41]

Some commentators, like the Dominican Claude Geffré, attribute much of the content of the Pastoral Constitution to Chenu, and while there are clear echoes of its themes in 'The Message to the World' in the sections of *Gaudium et Spes*, he was neither a member of the commission of Schema XIII nor did he meet with its membership. Congar records a number of meetings with Chenu during his involvement with the last revisions of Schema XIII but these are fleeting even if encouraging of his efforts. About Chenu's lecture on 'The Church of the Poor', Congar praised:

> A lecture by Chenu, a Chenu 200% better: intelligence, vitality, propheticism, presence. An analysis characterised by both a proheticism and an intellectual rigour that were sensational.[42]

Congar provided the theological anthropological basis to the first section of Schema XIII. But he did experience repeated rejection of his more prophetic insights. He reports in detail the varied critical responses to this material by Rahner, Ratzinger, Haubtmann, Schillebeeckx, Daniélou, Moeller and Phillips (among others). He commented how his own reaction to the document's drafts had shifted: 'then a more critical [phase], when I was more aware of the lack of synthesis in the area of anthropology and Christology.'[43] He also was disappointed about the decision of the Commission on Schema XIII, largely led by Karol Wojtyla (Pope John Paul II), not to address atheism more thoroughly in itself not merely as an absence of faith.

---

41. Congar, *My Journal*, (20 November 1962), 196.
42. Congar, (13 November 1964) 675–676.
43. Congar, (17 September 1965), 779–780

> I insisted on the profound character of questions posed by
> atheism, on the profound sameness of method with that of
> ecumenism (if we are dealing with atheism as a spiritual
> world of values and not simply with the fact of abandonment),
> on the necessity of making the theologians and pastors of the
> Church sensitive concerning it.[44]

Chenu was at the meeting at the Secretariat for Non-Believers along
with Cardinal König, Rahner, Häring, Houtart. This appears to be one
of the few times that Chenu attended such a formal gathering on the
Schema. Later Congar observed a shift happening in the reception of
his, Chenu's and Lubac's theology: 'So the turn and the conversion to
these 'French' ideas, that some people dread so much, is under way.'[45]
Here we can sense the influence of the Mission of France and the
worker-priest controversy on the mission orientation of their ecclesiology and pastoral emphasis. On the last day of the Council when the
final documents were promulgated, Congar was able to allow himself
this admission of his significant contribution to the Council: 'Even at
the Council I was involved in a great deal of work, over and above a general influence of presence and spoken contributions.' But he attributes
this to God like the faithful theological 'clerk' he understood himself to
be: 'God has overwhelmed me. He has gifted me profusely, infinitely
beyond my absolutely non-existent merits.'[46] In this we hear an echo of
the humility of St Thomas Aquinas on the completion of his *Summa*.

Final Points

Significance of these two theologians' contribution is without doubt,
Congar's being the more evident. Congar's extraordinary output in
ecclesiology and ecumenical theology corresponded to the need of
the post-Vatican II Church to define itself in terms of its history and
in relation to other branches of Christianity.

Congar's diaries (and Chenu's shorter notes) offer detailed evidence of the workings of the Council and the disputes and resolutions that produced the final documents. The number of meetings
formal and informal, the immense number of names listed in both

---

44. Congar, (22 September 1965), 785.
45. Congar, (26 November 1965), 853.
46. Congar, (7 December 1965), 871.

diaries attest to the expanse of involvement in the Council's efforts. Komonchak's concept of the 'experience' of Vatican II is evidenced in these engagements that produced the final documents of 'the event'.

This gives some inkling of the consciousness of the presence of Holy Spirit in these proceedings, that there could be so much level of discourse, disagreement and amendment and yet a *communio* and concord was mostly achieved through this confidence in the Council's call to dialogue.

Chenu's efforts at the periphery of the Council Fathers' debates also indicates the breadth as well as the many layers of the Council. He was among the many theologians who gave lectures, ran seminars and talked with groups of bishops in the hours outside of the assemblies. With Congar he wrote regular commentaries and reports for the French journal *ICI* (*Information Catholique Internationale*) and other newspapers. The Council as 'event' and 'experience' was thereby shared well beyond its participant bishops.

Congar himself evidences extraordinary openness and patience with the criticisms and attacks on his contributions. Although he also expresses disappointment in the quality of some of the bishops' understanding of the theological content and the pastoral imperatives, he retains his overwhelming commitment to the process of revision and insistence on certain topics, eg the need to address atheism, not just as the abandonment of faith.[47] Congar's was a practical ecclesiology.

There is a revisionism that discards the centrality of the teaching of *Gaudium et Spes* as secondary to the great but compromise document of *Lumen Gentium*, the Constitution on the Church. *Gaudium et Spes* is thereby misrepresented as an unfortunate example of 1960's experimentation with the ecclesial equivalent of a 1960's 'hippie' consciousness. Rather, the Bishops' *Message to all people and nations* substantiates the historicity of the claim that the challenge of "the Church in the modern world" was not only pivotal to the *aggiornamento* but framed the Council's agenda and direction from the start. Chenu, especially, but Congar also, are often accused of an optimism that confines their theology to the enthusiasms of the 1960's, but this is to ignore their historical context. They lived through World War I and World War II, the Nazi Occupation of France, being a prisoner of war in the infamous Colditz prison, the Cold War and the threat

---

47. Congar, (21 September 1965), 785.

of Atomic annihilation, AND the repeated condemnations they had lived under from the Church's authorities. Rather than an optimism theirs is an eschatologically oriented confidence in God.

Congar was both inside and outside the Council. While he contributed so substantially within the workings of the Council, both he and Chenu were directed by their orientation to dialogue outside with the world.

A final story apt to some of today's struggles with the ownership of the interpretation of Vatican II. On 15 September 1965, Congar favourably records at that day's Mass one of the liturgical reforms being introduced: 'An interesting innovation: the celebrant entered carrying the Book of the Gospels during the processional Psalm'.[48] In his diary Chenu reports a wicked suggestion by one of the Salesian bishops, Bishop Naumann, in regard to the lively complaints that this procession of the Word was to the detriment of the other ecclesial 'source' *Tradition*. The bishop suggested this could be corrected by representing Tradition through pushing Cardinal Ottaviani down St Peter's nave on a tea-trolley.[49]

Chenu and Consecratio mundi

Chenu's contribution is perhaps most evident in the controversy produced by his objection to the use of the phrase '*consecratio mundi*' in *Lumen gentium* (no. 34).[50] Chenu wrote on the subject, first in 1964 and twice in 1966, after the close of the Council.[51] At issue for him was

---

48. Congar, (15 September 1965), 775.
49. Chenu, *Notes quotidiennes au Concile*,119.
50. The final version of *Lumen gentium* (no. 34) was: 'Sic et laici, qua adoratores ubique sancte agentes, ipsum mundum Deo consecrant.' (in Latin) and 'De cette manière, les laïcs, en une sainte et universelle adoration, consacrent à Dieu le monde même.' (in French). The concept of '*consecratio mundi*' was changed to 'to consecrate the world'. See Protais Safi, 'La «consecratio mundi» et la théologie du laïcat à la veille de Vatican II' (unpublished STD thesis, Lateran Pontifical University, Rome, 1981).
51. '«Consecratio mundi»', *Nouvelle Revue Théologique* 86 (1964): 608–18; which was expanded upon in 'Les Laïcs et la «consecratio mundi»' Guilherme Baraúna OFM and Y.M.-J. Congar OP. (eds.), *L'Église de Vatican II* (*Unam Sanctam* 51c, tome III), (Paris: Les Éditions du Cerf, 1966), pp. 1035–1053. A further version appeared in 1966 as 'Les Laïcs et la «consécration» du monde' in *Peuple de Dieu dans le monde* (Paris: Cerf, 1966), pp. 69–96.

the integrity of the lay apostolate not to be understood as a crypto-priesthood in a theocratic worldview, and the inherent goodness and autonomy of creation.[52] Chenu further declared that the feared desacralisation of the world, because of secularisation and the rise of atheism among the masses, was actually deeply Christian because, like Christ's defeat of the demons, it demystified the false gods and demons and their hold on human consciousness.[53] The role of the Church in the world was not to consecrate it, because the Incarnation had declared that 'la distinction entre profane et sacré est dissoute.'[54] Therefore it is in the construction of the world, not its consecration, that the Church and its laity are properly engaged.

Chenu identified that '*consecratio mundi*' bore significance well beyond its intended use and would seem to counter the Church's involvement in the world as developed in *Gaudium et spes*.[55] Chenu's objection to '*consecratio mundi*' represents most fully the anthropological priority in his ecclesiology as through it he emphasised the inherent value of the humanity of the laity and how the mission of the Church is best effected through the witness of this humanity, rather than in an increase of sacralised ministers imported into the world with some vague sacramentalising capacity for announcing its salvation. Chenu instead insisted that it was the humanity of the laity that revealed most profoundly the mystery of the Incarnation to fellow humans and the immersion of these Christians in the 'profane' world reproduced most faithfully the condition of Christ on earth. This constituted a theological re-positioning not only of the role of the laity in the Church's mission, but of mission itself and of the Church's affirmation of the humanity it exists to serve.

---

52. Much later Chenu described this in terms of the Church's liturgy before Vatican II: 'La liturgie était un phénomène aristocratique réservé aux moines.' *Un théologien en liberté*, p. 92.
53. pp. 612–613.
54. p. 616.
55. pp. 74–5.

InterfaceTheology 3/1 2017

Cardijn and Congar at Vatican II

Stefan Gigacz

Introduction

'I was ordained a priest on 25 July 1930. From that moment, the Young Christian Workers (movement) became a heartfelt cause for me', wrote Yves Congar in a 1975 letter to Marguerite Fiévez, archivist of the movement's founder Joseph Cardijn.[1]

Soon after, by now teaching and researching at the Dominican study centre, *Le Saulchoir*, at Kain near Tournai in Belgium, he would begin to preach retreats to leaders of the YCW.

A little later, he would meet Cardijn himself, beginning a working relationship and friendship that would last until the Second Vatican Council when Cardijn, now a Cardinal with a global profile, asked Congar, who had also become a theologian of world renown, to assist him in preparing his conciliar speeches.

This paper traces the story of that partnership from the 'golden age' of the YCW in France and Belgium during the 1930s, through the challenging and dark days of the late 1940s and 1950s when tensions over the worker priests led to Congar's 'exile' first to Cambridge and then to Strasbourg, and finally to the years of triumph at the Council.

---

1. « J'ai été ordonné prêtre le 25 juillet 1930. Dès ce moment, la JOC a été pour moi une cause chère. » Letter to Cardijn's archivist and former secretary, Marguerite Fiévez, 22 October 1975. Translation of this and other unpublished texts into English by myself. Cardijn Archives, Brussels, 1970.

The 'Golden Age' of the YCW 1925–1939

The Saulchoir at Kain

The Saulchoir study centre was established at Kain in an old Cistercian abbey in 1904 following the expulsions from France of Catholic religious.[2] By the time that Congar arrived there as a student in late 1926,[3] it was already a well-established intellectual bridge between Belgium and France.

Moreover, it was a study centre whose "historical" approach to theology and philosophy would soon become problematic in the eyes of the Holy See and lead to its eventual transfer back to France. Probably no-one has better described this ethos of the Saulchoir than Congar's close friend and elder, Fr MD Chenu:

'Our decisive approach is this: the theologian is he who dares to speak humanly of the Word of God.'[4]

As Chenu wrote in his controversial book on the Saulchoir, this implied being "present in our time," words that would echo through to Vatican II and beyond.

"Theologically speaking," Chenu wrote, "this means being present to the facts revealed in the present life of the Church and the current experience of Christendom."[5]

And the Dominicans of the Saulchoir were very deeply involved in both the life of the Church and the world of that period. Among the masters Congar would meet at Le Saulchoir was the philosopher AD Sertillanges,[6] thomist philosopher, who had been close to the Sillon, the pioneering lay movement created by Marc Sangnier that would become the prototype for the YCW and other Specialised Catholic Action movements. In 1916, Sertillanges had already published his major work *La philosophie morale de Saint Thomas d'Aquin* which

---

2. MD Chenu, *Une école de théologie, Le Théologie* (Kain-lez-Tournai – Etiolles: Le Saulchoir, 1937), 32.
3. Jean Puyo and Yves Congar, *Une vie pour la vérité, Jean Puyo interroge le Père Congar* (Paris: Centurion, 1975), 30.
4. « Nous voici à la démarche décisive : le théologien est celui qui ose parler humainement la Parole de Dieu. » Chenu, *Une école de théologie*, 69–70.
5. « Être présent à son temps, disions-nous. Nous y voici. Théologiquement parlant, c'est être présent au donné révélé dans la vie présente de l'Église et l'expérience actuelle de la Chrétienté. » Chenu, *Une école de théologie*, 67.
6. AD Sertillanges, *La philosophie morale de Saint Thomas d'Aquin* (Paris: Felix Alcan, 1916).

would contribute greatly to providing a philosophical foundation to Cardijn's see-judge-act method.

Indeed, the French Dominicans during the 1930s were a hotbed of former Sillon activists including the jurists Georges Renard and Joseph Delos, who would eventually also become a peritus at Vatican II. Another Dominican, the Belgian Ceslas Rutten, who had been Cardijn's superior in charge of social work in the Malines archdiocese, went to work in a coal mine for three months as part of an enquiry into worker conditions and may also have been involved in an abortive project to introduce the Sillon in Brussels.

In such a context of enthusiasm for social action, it was almost inevitable that the newly ordained Yves Congar would seek out the YCW almost as soon as he was ordained.

Preaching retreats to the YCW

In fact, as a 1936 article by MD Chenu, *La JOC au Saulchoir*, makes clear by 1933 the Dominican community had already committed to work closely with the YCW and the emerging 'Specialised Catholic Action' movements.

Chenu himself had been in contact with the YCW since 1928 when chaplains from the new YCW in the Lille region began to cross the border to reflect at the Saulchoir where Chenu was in charge of hosting them.[7] From that time, the Dominicans launched regular retreats for these movements in Paris and Lille in France as well as the Saulchoir in Belgium.[8]

---

7. Jacque Duquesne and MD Chenu, *Un théologien en liberté, Jacques Duquesne interroge le Père Chenu* (Paris: Centurion, 1975), 57.

8. « Il ne s'agissait pas seulement, en effet, de recevoir quelques amateurs de silence et d'émotion claustrale, mais bien de faire participer effectivement, par la liturgie et par la doctrine, des groupes de laïcs à la vie spirituelle—à la vie tout court—d'un couvent dominicain. C'est dans ce contexte que, depuis trois ans, se sont établies des retraites, individuelles ou collectives, à l'usage des « mouvements spécialisés », très particulièrement à l'usage de la J.O.C. dans ses divers éléments, dirigeants, militants, propagandistes, aumôniers surtout. Rencontre trop naturelle pour qu'on n'y voie pas une garantie réciproque de bon travail. » MD Chenu, *La JOC au Saulchoir*, in *La Parole de Dieu II, L'Evangile dans le temps,* Cogitatio Fidei Series (Paris: Cerf, 1964), 271–274. In fact, Congar's first retreats for the YCW were held in November 1932. See below.

> It was not just a matter of receiving a few amateurs in cloistered silence and emotion but of truly enabling groups of lay people to effectively participate, through the liturgy and doctrine in the whole life of a Dominican convent. It was in this context that for the last three years individual and collective retreats were established for the benefit of the 'specialised movements', particularly the benefit of the YCW," Chenu wrote in May 1936.[9]

Later this work expanded into the organisation of full blown retreats for the chaplains and leaders of the YCW.

Referring specifically to the Saulchoir, Chenu noted that 'three fathers devoted themselves regularly' to the work with the YCW in Paris, in the North of France and 'once or twice with those from the (YCW) general secretariat in Brussels'. Although he does not name them, it is likely that the three fathers are himself, Congar and Father Henri Féret. 'We were a trio', Congar later commented.[10]

It is therefore clear that young Father Congar's choice to become involved with the YCW was part of a community commitment by the Dominicans of that time. 'I preached many retreats', Congar said much later, adding that Chenu himself often took part in these meetings.

He also kept a systematic list of all the retreats that he preached as well as the correspondence and even photos relating to them. Indeed, a list of some twenty-eight retreats from 1932–1938 given by Congar to YCW leaders from the Belgian cities of Tournai and Mouscron as well as from Lille and Tourcoing across the border in France is still to be found in his personal archives, along with the actual retreat notes

---

9.   « Dans les six derniers mois, ont eu lieu, pour les aumôniers, la retraite annuelle d'une douzaine d'aumôniers de Paris, puis six récollections mensuelles des aumôniers du Nord, auxquels se joignent une fois ou l'autre ceux du secrétariat général de Bruxelles. Trois Pères se consacrent régulièrement au groupe (organisation générale, conférences spirituelles avec discussions, entretiens personnels). » MD Chenu, *La JOC au Saulchoir*, in *La Parole de Dieu II, L'Evangile dans le temps* (Paris: Cogitatio Fidei Series, Cerf, 1964), 271–274. Originally published in *L'année dominicaine* (May 1936): 190–193.

10.   Puyo – Congar, *Une vie pour la vérité*, 45.

on themes such as prayer, faith, the priesthood of the faithful, the Eucharist, as well as secular themes such as work, life, etc.[11]

'We received YCW groups for retreats from Saturday afternoon to Sunday evening YCW groups', Congar wrote, and the schedules were quite demanding.

After a Saturday evening orientation session, there was sometimes Night Adoration at midnight for half an hour. Wake up call the next morning was at 5.30am, followed by Mass and recollection from 6.00am to 7.15am, then breakfast and recreation, with Rosary and reflection at 8.00am, followed by High Mass at 9.00am with the program finishing on Sunday afternoon at around 4.00pm!

Not surprisingly the young YCW leaders, who were often around fifteen to sixteen years of age, were a little dubious initially.

'The first time, the young jocists from Mouscron, a small Belgian city near Tourcoing, were not very convinced', Congar reminisced. 'A convent! What are we doing here? But they found them so good that they often came back.'

'The retreats took place in a fervent atmosphere', he added. 'I spoke to the jocists about the Gospel; they questioned me. I made an effort to meet them in their concrete difficulties.'

Thus, Congar's notes are peppered with references to 'the factory', 'the street, at leisure' and 'the family', namely the various places in which apostolic action was to be developed. 'Religion is life', says Congar in one of his retreat notes.

One of these notes cites Cardijn's own definition of prayer as a "study circle with God," a striking quote that would probably have been lost to history if not recorded by Congar. It is also evident from Congar's notes that some of the retreat outlines that had been prepared by the YCW chaplains, probably by Cardijn himself.

---

11. The first retreats for the JOC are dated 6 November 1932, 20 November 1932 (location illegible), 27 November 1932 (JOC d'Antoing) and then Christmas 1932. In 1933, retreats took place on 5 March (JOC Tournai), 12 March (JOC Mouscron), 12–14 August (JOC Mouscron, militants), 7–8 October (JOC Mouscron, dirigeants et militants), 15–16 October (dirigeants et militants), 4 November (pré-jocistes Mouscron), 31 December (Sermon à Mouscron aux jocistes).

Congar's impact on the young workers

The YCW leaders also seem to have been impressed by the intensity of these sessions. However, on one occasion a chaplain from Mouscron was moved to write to warn Congar that the following retreat group was much younger and that he needed to prepare a lighter program with half an hour's recreation 'after lunch, after Mass, and even after supper!'[12]

Despite Congar's early fears, most YCW leaders clearly appreciated these retreats, which also give an insight into what a dynamic preacher and personality he was, long before illness confined him to a wheelchair.

'They left raring to go on Sunday evening', Congar said. 'We could hear them singing from several hundred metres away towards the Tournai station, which was three kilometres away from the Saulchoir.'

Thanking Congar for one retreat and requesting a follow up meeting for his 'comrades', one Mouscron YCW leader, Raphaël Lecroart, described their own recent retreat as 'a genuine treat for our young people.'

'All without exception were amazed and enthused. We can ask them any small sacrifice now. It's enough simply to remind them occasionally of the resolutions they made during their retreat', Lecroart wrote.[13]

Nor did he hesitate to seek Congar's help with a problem, namely 'the sudden and incomprehensible disappearance of Louis (our president)'.

'I don't know what has happened inside his head but he refuses to give us any explanation. Could I ask you a great service? Quite simply come to our aid. Pray for him, write to him', Lecroart asked.[14]

---

12. *Letter from Jos. Vereecke to Congar*, 19 October 1933. Congar Archives.
13. « La dernière recollection pour les jeunes fut une véritable régal. Tous indistinctement, furent emerveillés, enthousiasmés. Et on peut demander n'importe quel petit sacrifice. Il suffit pour cela de leur rappeler de temps à autre les résolutions prises en récollection. » *Letter from Raphaël Lecroart* to Congar, undated. Congar Archives.
14. « Mais un fait plus saillant à vous signaler: La défaillance soudaine et incompréhensible de Louis (notre président). Je ne sais ce qui lui passe par la tête mais il nous refuse . . . le moindre explication. Je me permets de vous demander un grand service. Tout simplement de venir à notre secours. Priez pour lui, écrivez lui. » *Letter from Raphaël Lecroart to Congar.*

Although there is no record of Congar's response, there is little doubt that it would have been rapid and forthcoming.

Another young soldier wrote to Congar asking him to be his spiritual director.[15]

One YCW chaplain was so impressed with the impact of Congar's retreats on his YCW leaders that he wrote to Congar asking if he could also organise a similar retreat for local priests.[16]

But not everything always went to plan.

'It is truly with sadness that I learnt how few jocists took to heart this retreat that you agreed to preach to them. Please allow me to present my apologies but I must say that never has such disorder reigned in my regional federation', wrote Léon Debruyne to Congar in August 1933.[17]

Moreover he does not hesitate to take Congar to task.

'In your desire to do good for the souls of my worker comrades, you allowed them to abuse your hospitality. You asked too little for the expenses of their stay. They broke a chamber pot (and perhaps other things that I don't know about) but you did not ask them to reimburse the cost', Debruyne continued.[18]

Congar clearly took the lesson to heart and in the next retreats, he very carefully, if politely, laid down the law of retreats, beginning with an exhortation based on the following notes:

'Spirit and conditions of this retreat. Deepen their Christian life by making an experience of complete Christian life. To play the game deeply and sincerely . . . order, silence . . .'. Congar wrote, recalling the objectives that the Dominicans had fixed for these retreats.[19]

---

15. Noël Callens, *Undated letter to Congar*, probably late 1933. Congar Archives.
16. *Letter from Jos Vereecke to Congar*, 9 October 1933. Congar Archives.
17. « C'est vraiment avec tristesse que j'ai appris combien peu de jocistes ont pris à cœur cette retraite que vous avez voulu bien leur prêcher. Aussi, permettez-moi de vous présenter mes excuses, mais je dois vous dire que jamais pareille désordre n'a régné dans ma fédé. » *Letter from Léon Debruyne to Congar,* 21 August 1933. Congar Archives.
18. « Dans votre désir de faire le bien aux âmes de mes camarades ouvriers, vous avez laissé abuser de votre bonté. Vous leurs avez demandés trop peu pour les frais de séjour. Ils ont cassé un vase de nuit et vous n'avez réclamé aucune indemnité et peut-être autre chose que j'ignore. » *Letter from Léon Debruyne to Congar.*
19. « Esprit et conditions de cette retraite. Approfondir leur vie chrétienne en faisant une expérience de vie chrétienne complète. Pour jouer . . . à fond et sincèrement le jeu . . . ordre, silence, etc. » Undated notes of another retreat. Congar Archives.

Cardijn, Congar and the Dominicans

It was through these retreats that Congar soon came into contact with Cardijn himself.

'Very soon I met the founder of the YCW, Canon Cardijn and his assistant, Fr Robert Kothen', Congar told an interviewer much later.[20] But although he visited the famous Jociste Centrale[21] in Boulevard Poincaré in central Brussels, his contact was more frequent with Kothen,[22] who was responsible for international contacts of the YCW.

Nevertheless, Cardijn's influence was critical, particularly his speech *Ite Missa Est* delivered at Reims on 26 July 1933 during the French Semaine Sociale,[23] in which he emphasised the importance of bringing faith and sacraments to the radiating circles of the life of each person, their local environment or milieu as well as to the masses.[24]

It is very likely also that Congar accompanied Chenu to Cardijn's extraordinary mass to mark the 10th anniversary of the YCW held before a crowd of 100,000 people at Heysel Stadium on 25 August 1935. Chenu later recounted the story of the Dominicans who

---

20. Puyo – Congar, *Une vie pour la vérité*, 52.
21. The multi-storey former textile factory that Cardijn had asked for and received free of charge from a leading industrial family. Marguerite Fiévez, Jacques Meert with the collaboration of Roger Aubert (Preface, Helder Camara), *Cardijn* (London: Young Christian Workers, undated), 100–103.
22. Jacques Leclerq, *L'abbé Robert Kothen, Une vie de prêtre* (Namur: Editions du Soleil Levant, 1958), 45 et s.
23. « De Cardijn j'ai particulièrement aimé sa conférence de la Semaine sociale de Reims, « Ita Missa est ». » Congar, *Letter to Marguerite Fiévez*, 22 October 1975. http://priests.josephcardijn.com/testimony-on-cardijn (Accessed 12/03/2019)
24. « Il faut considérer la vie réelle voulue par Dieu dans laquelle il n'y a rien d'artificiel et chercher comment cette vie-là glorifiera Dieu. C'est cette vie-là dont il faut faire la vraie Messe, prolongement de la messe du prêtre, offrande unie à celle du Rédempteur à travers le temps et l'espace, de façon que les jeunes travailleurs deviennent les membres conscients et volontaires de ce grand corps mystique que doit devenir l'humanité tout entière pour rendre ainsi gloire à Dieu son Créateur et Rédempteur . . . Pour un nombre immense de chrétiens, la religion est une affaire privée, séparée de leur vie journalière, alors qu'elle doit être l'âme, le moteur, le transformateur, le surnaturalisateur de toute cette vie. La religion a cela comme but. C'est toute la vie qui doit être religieuse, qui doit chanter « Gloria in excelsis Deo » » Cardijn, *Ite Missa Est* http://www.josephcardijn.fr/1933---ite-missa-est (Accessed 12/03/2019)

attended the event.[25] A Belgian parish priest looked accusingly at their white soutanes and said: 'Oh, you intellectuals . . . you are so distant from the YCW!' But the YCW leaders defended the Dominicans against their 'bourgeois' critic!

Thus, Cardijn clearly made a huge impact on young Congar. In *Vraies et fausses réformes de l'Eglise*, the theologian was moved to compare Cardijn's historic first meeting with Pope Pius XI in 1925, which led to the approval of the YCW despite the lingering doubts of Malines Cardinal Désiré Mercier, with the way in which medieval popes had taken the emerging movements of St Francis and St Dominic under their pontifical wing.

> The creation of the YCW is one of the most emblematic events of our time, in which we find a prophetic initiative from the periphery, whereby a curate from suburban Brussels arrives in Rome with a letter from his archbishop and receives the consecration from the pope, himself also animated with a prophetic spirit, by which the young movement becomes a movement of the Church itself, the prototype of the reforming creations of Catholic Action.[26]

Indeed, Congar went so far as to credit the YCW and its sister movement of Specialised Catholic Action as having played a decisive role in reforming the Church of that period.

---

25. « Au récent congrès mondial de la J.O.C. (Bruxelles, juin 1935), un brave homme de curé, rencontrant quatre ou cinq robes blanches au milieu d'un groupe de jeunesse ouvrière, laissa échapper naïvement ce propos : « Ah! vous, les intellectuels . . ., vous êtes bien loin de la J.O.C.! » Ce furent les jocistes qui se chargèrent de riposter à ce bon « bourgeois ». » Chenu, *La JOC au Saulchoir*, 1936 in Chenu 1964, 273.

26. « La création de la J.O.C. en constituerait, de nos jours, l'un des plus symptomatiques : où nous aurions l'initiative, périphérique et prophétique s'il en est, d' un vicaire de la banlieue de Bruxelles, qui se rend à Rome muni d'une lettre de son archevêque et là rencontre, de la part d'un pape qu'animait, lui aussi, l'esprit prophétique, une consécration par laquelle le jeune mouvement devient un mouvement de l'Eglise elle-même, le prototype des créations réformatrices de l'Action catholique. Magnifique création, ouverture pleine de promesses du développement : œuvre prophétique née du double prophétisme conjugué de la périphérie et du centre. » Yves Congar, *Vrai et fausse réforme dans l'Eglise* (Paris: Cerf, 1950), 282–285.

> In France, everything arose from a realisation, ultimately completely realistic, of the true apostolic situation . . . From 1925 to 1940, within the Catholic Action framework, there was the practice of the enquiry method. With their 'guys' and 'girls', priests became aware of the questions raised within the 'milieu'; they also learnt to better appreciate the objections, the problems, the understandings, the distractions, the real state of the milieu from which their formation, their dignity, their priestly functions had cut them off. This unleashed a new impulse. I well remember the jocist study circles and the workshops of that time.[27]

This also led to a progressive deepening of the relationship of the Dominicans with Cardijn and the YCW going far beyond the holding of retreats.

In 1936, the French Dominican provincial Fr Padé made an agreement with Cardijn to release two priests, Fathers Albert Bouché and Bernard Rouzet, to work with the French YCW. In fact, Fr Bouché had already spent several weeks in 1933 working in a coal mine in Charleroi, Belgium. And both Bouché and Rouzet had worked in factories during their summer holidays while students.

Both priests rapidly became regional YCW chaplains as they sought to find their way as 'missionnaires de travail' missionaries of the workplace, an experience that would soon blossom into the worker priest movement.[28]

The impact of Cardijn and the YCW on Congar's theology

As he acknowledged many times, Congar learnt much from these encounters with Cardijn and the YCW. 'I owe a lot to those young

---

27. « Causes spécifiques. Elles seules ont été vraiment décisives. Tout est venu, en France, d'une prise de conscience enfin pleinement réaliste de la véritable situation apostolique. Celle-ci s'est opérée en deux temps. De 1925 à 1940, il y a eu, dans le cadre de l'Action catholique dont ces quinze années furent le beau printemps, la pratique de la méthode d'enquête. Avec leurs « gars » et leurs « filles », les prêtres ont reçu les questions posées par le « milieu » ; ils ont mieux connu les objections, les problèmes, les lectures, les distractions, l'état réel du milieu dont leur formation, leur dignité, leurs fonctions cultuelles les tenaient coupés. Cela a suscité un bel élan. Je me rappelle les cercles d'études jocistes, les chapitres routiers de cette période. » Yves Congar, *op. cit.*, 46–49.

28. François Leprieur, *Quand Rome condamne* (Paris: Plon/Cerf, 1989), 23.

guys. They taught me what it means to implant the Gospel in humanity', he explained.[29]

'At the Saulchoir, we were a little preserved from the danger (of
being intellectually isolated from the lives and struggles of ordinary
people) thanks to men like Fr Chenu, who was so gifted for contact
with his contemporaries and more courageous than I am. Thanks
equally to our relations with the YCW (Young Christian Workers).
These links were decisive for me. I have always believed in dialogue
between the theological and the pastoral', Congar explained later,
particularly in orienting his future work as a theologian.[30]

All this evidently had a great impact on Congar's own theological
approach.

'The (YCW) consciousness', Congar explained,[31] entered into sym-
biosis with the theology of the mystical body that we find simplified,
for example, in the books of Fr Glorieux, and which led to a spirituality of 'incarnation'.

'The young workers continued the life of Christ the Worker. Their
life at work was like a "continuing incarnation", a theme that could
lead to ambiguity but which Fr Chenu helped us to interpret in terms
of realism and the grace of the Word.'

Moreover, it was at that time Congar wrote, 'that I took up the
habit of linking the doxology which ends the Canon of the Mass –
"by Him, with Him and in Him"—to this incarnation of Christ in
the human dough. A vision that I enlarged in a Teilhardian, if you
like—I have been a Teilhardian in the technical sense of the word, but
I totally agree with his cosmological and Christological vision, which
seems to me to be authentically Paulinian.

"Thus, I owe to the YCW and to our meetings with the worker
chaplains in Lille—among whom I knew Fr (Henri) Godin, one of the
authors of *La France, pays de mission?*—the notion (which would cer-

---

29. Puyo – Congar, *Une vie pour la vérité*, 52.
30. Puyo – Congar, *Une vie pour la vérité*, 41.
31. « Cette conscience entrait en symbiose avec la théologie du Corps mystique telle
    qu'on la trouve vulgarisée, par exemple, dans les livres de P. Glorieux, ce qui
    aboutissait à une spiritualité d'« incarnation » Les jeunes travailleurs continuaient
    la vie du Christ-ouvrier. Leur vie de travail constituait' comme une « incarnation
    continuée » : un thème qui pouvait prêter à l'ambiguïté mais que le P. Chenu nous
    aidait à interpréter en termes de réalisme de la grâce et de la Parole. » Congar,
    Ministères et communions ecclésiales (Paris: Cerf, 1971), 11–13.

tainly require nuancing) of the Mystical Body of Christ in the workshop', Congar wrote.[32]

'Fr Chenu developed this theme in many articles: the Word of God, and grace are incarnated in humanity, humanity taken in its historical dimension, its becoming, its dynamism; in its social dimension, insists Fr Chenu, in its conditions of class struggle, in the movements of liberation.'

Meanwhile, Congar the theologian continued to work on the 1937 book that would become his landmark work on ecumenical relations, *Chrétiens désunis*. In this book, he cites the YCW as part of the movement of reform that he saw already under way within the Church encompassing liturgy, lay apostolate, missionary and ecumenical activity—all themes that would be specifically addressed by Vatican II:

'Let us be clear', Congar wrote.

> The movement that began under Pius X, concerning which the war changed a few points of implementation but did not break the continuity, and which has found its own formula, namely *Instaurare omnia in Christo*, is a movement of reform. A movement of reform in liturgy, a movement of reform in the missionary effort launched by Benedict XV and developed under the leadership of Pius XI; a movement of reform movement in Catholic Action, participation of the laity in the apostolate of the hierarchy; and in Catholic Action, even more particularly in the magnificent achievement of the YCW.[33]

---

32. Puyo – Congar, *Une vie pour la vérité*, 53.

33. « Il ne faut pas s'y tromper : le mouvement commencé sous Pie X, dont la guerre a pu changer quelques points d'application, mais non briser la continuité, et qui a trouvé sa formule dans l'Instaurare omnia in Christo, est un mouvement de réforme. Mouvement de réforme que le mouvement liturgique; mouvement de réforme que l'effort missionnaire inauguré par Benoît XV et développé sous l'impulsion de Pie XI ; mouvement de réforme que l'Action catholique, participation du laïcat à l'apostolat hiérarchique, et, dans l'Action catholique, plus spécialement encore, la réalisation magnifique de la JOC ; mouvement de réforme que ce renouvellement intérieur de la théologie catholique actuelle dans le sens d'un contact plus sérieux avec les sources, d'une moins complète ignorance de la tradition orientale . . . que cette valeur nouvelle d'interprétation ou de réponse, cette reprise de l'initiative intellectuelle et cette liberté de la pensée dont les catholiques font preuve en histoire, en philosophie, en sociologie, en culture, en art. » Yves Congar, *Chrétiens désunis: Principes d'un 'oecuménisme' catholique* (Paris: Cerf, 1937), 339–340.

This effectively sums up Congar's attitude to the 'golden age' of the YCW in Belgium and Francd as "an enthusiastic youth, conscious of carrying the cause of evangelical witness in the worker milieu."[34]

The 'dark years': 1940–1958

Rays of hope amid the fog of war

Nevertheless, clouds were also gathering—war clouds as well as theological clouds.

Trouble was already brewing at the Saulchoir over Chenu's 1937 book *Le Saulchoir, Une école de théologie*, which explained the centre's then-controversial "historical" approach to theology. In a sense, the Saulchoir method was little more than an adaptation of the empirical fact-based method used by the YCW to the field of theology. Indeed, Chenu referred approvingly to the YCW in the book.[35] But this did not satisfy the Holy See which placed the book on the *Index librorum prohibitorum* in 1942.

Meanwhile, as Congar recounts, the Saulchoir moved back to France arriving on 2 September 1939, the very eve of the outbreak of World War II. He therefore spent only one week at the new convent at Etiolles near Paris, before being mobilised as a lieutenant in the French Army. Two days of combat in 1940 led to his capture by the advancing Germans and his internment at Colditz as a prisoner of war for the duration of the conflict.[36]

On the other hand, the German occupation of France failed to shake a rising concern over the failure of the Church to reach out to the industrial working class. Thus, the Dominican Jacques Loew, started working on the docks at Marseilles in 1941. By 1944, Loew and his colleagues had obtained the support of local Archbishop Jean Delay

34. « C'était une jeunesse enthousiaste, consciente de porter, dans le milieu ouvrier, la cause du témoignage évangélique. » Congar, *Ministères*, 11–13.
35. « Le Saulchoir a eu, ces années passées, la joie et la grâce de recevoir régulièrement aumôniers et militants de la J. O. C., qui font de ce couvent, tout occupé de livres et de théologie intemporelle, l'un de leurs lieux spirituels les plus aimés et les plus sûrs. C'est pour des « théologiens » un inappréciable critère de leur présence, que cette rencontre spontanée avec la J. O. C. et ses pareils; ils voient là un témoignage de l'authenticité chrétienne et de la vitalité surnaturelle de leur austère travail théologique. » Chenu, *Le Saulchoir*, 68–69.
36. Puyo – Congar, *Une vie pour la vérité*, 85.

to establish a community of life oriented to working with the Catholic Action movements in the working-class suburbs of the port city.[37]

The Dominican-published 1943 book *La France, pays de mission?*[38] by Godin and Yvan Daniel (with a preface by French YCW founding chaplain, Georges Guérin) caused a huge stir. Its very title raised the question as to whether France—still the eldest daughter of the Church in the minds of many Catholics—had become a 'mission' country.

Cardinal Emmanuel Suhard of Paris, who had already motivated the French bishops to launch a seminary for worker priests in 1942 which eventually led to the creation of the 'Mission de France', was deeply shaken by the book's findings, which were presented as the results of an empirical YCW-style enquiry. Godin and Daniel had recommended two major thrusts of action to deal with the problem, namely the development of 'communities' that would go beyond the traditional parishes, and the development of the 'worker priest' approach.

Tragically, Godin, a Paris diocesan priest, did not live to see the creation of his 'Mission de Paris', dying in an electrical accident on the very eve of its foundation in January 1943. But his life and even his death deeply impressed Congar who later wrote that 'once more, by simply endeavouring to be true, a man pronounced the words that so many others needed to hear'.[39]

'It was not just his death that sealed the work of Fr Godin with the very seal of the cross, a divine cachet of authenticity. The man and his work were truly providential,' Congar wrote.[40]

---

37. Jacques Loew, *Journal d'une Mission ouvrière* (Paris, Series Livres de Vie, Cerf, 1959), 17.

38. The book was published in 1943 by the Dominicans in Paris by 'Les Editions du Cerf' and at Lyon by the wartime publishing house 'Les Editions de l'Abeille'.

39. « Il n'est pas jusqu'à sa mort qui n'ait mis sur l'œuvre de l'abbé Godin, avec le sceau même de la croix, un cachet d'authenticité divine. L'homme et l'œuvre étaient vraiment providentiels, prophétique ». Yves Congar, *Vrai et fausse réforme dans l'Eglise*, 46–49.

40. « *La France, pays de mission?* des abbés Godin et Daniel, paraissait en 1943. L'épisode est désormais bien connu, je ne le raconterai pas; on peut même dire qu'il appartient à l'Histoire. Une fois de plus, en s'appliquant simplement à être vrai, un homme prononçait les paroles que tant d'autres avaient besoin d'entendre. Il n'est pas jusqu'à sa mort qui n'ait mis sur l'œuvre de l'abbé Godin, avec le sceau même de la croix, un cachet d'authenticité divine. L'homme et l'œuvre étaient vraiment providentiels, prophétique ». On a beaucoup travaillé depuis ; le visage apostolique ou missionnaire de l'Eglise s'est affermi ou même transformé. Très vite, ce travail a mené à une prise de conscience nouvelle de la situation du monde et du rapport de l'Eglise à ce monde. » *Ibid.*

By the time that Congar returned from the war in 1945, the Dominicans had thrown themselves even more deeply into the development of the worker priest network. For Congar, the situation was full of hope.

'Towards 46–47, we experienced some quite exceptional moments in an ecclesial climate of rediscovered freedom and liberation, and marvellous creativity on the pastoral level', Congar said later concerning these new initiatives.[41]

But, as the fate of Chenu's book illustrated, Rome was already raising its eyebrows over 'the application of sociology to the Christian religion'.

'We can situate the first manifestations of concern by Rome towards the end of summer 1947', Congar said. 'We began to receive a series of warnings, then threats concerning the worker priests. I began to be refused permission from my superiors and I could not take part in the 1948 Amsterdam ecumenical meeting.'

Congar and the rise of the international lay apostolate movements

Congar turned forty in 1945 as the war ended. By this time there was also a new post-war generation of YCW leaders emerging. So it was quite natural that Congar's personal contacts with the YCW would become more sporadic.

On the other hand, the involvement of the Dominicans with the worker priests brought them into closer contact with other movements such as the Action Catholique Ouvrière (ACO), the adult equivalent of the YCW, in which many former YCW leaders were also involved.

Congar thus soon began to receive a growing number of invitations to address a variety of events, particularly chaplains meetings, including those of the YCW, YCS, Rural YCW as well as the ACO, the Catholic Intellectuals and other lay movements.[42]

---

41. Puyo – Congar, *Une vie pour la vérité*, 98.
42. Congar's archives list talks given to the JEC (YCS), JAC (Rural YCW), ACO, the Catholic Intellectual Movement and may other lay movements and organisations. Several of these talks are reproduced in his *Sacerdoce et Laïcat* (Yves Congar, *Sacerdoce et Laïcat devant leurs tâches d'évangélisation et civilisation* (Paris: Cerf, 1962).

He also began to write more systematically on the theology of the laity including in *Masses ouvrières*, a magazine of the ACO as well as in theological journals.[43]

However, with growing suspicion in Rome of the worker priest movement, it was natural also that doubts would also emerge concerning the work of the YCW. By this time, the YCW had spread to more than fifty countries and was facing new challenges of its own. As soon as the war was ended, Cardijn had recommenced his habit of annual visits to the Vatican to meet with the Pope.

Now it was no longer Pius XI who had given his approval to the movement in 1925 but Pius XII. In his first meeting with Cardijn in May 1946, the Pius XII added his approval.

'Our desire is that the YCW be set up everywhere', he told Cardijn.[44]

'But we want a YCW like your own', the Pope continued in a significant gloss on his approval, implying that perhaps not all YCWs were like Cardijn's YCW. Was this a reference to the situation in France and the worker priests?

Cardijn himself apparently harboured early doubts about the French worker priest experience even though he greatly appreciated the book of Godin and Daniel.

'Cardijn appreciated the values of this experience and the new possibilities it opened up, as a contribution to solving the problem which, forty years earlier, he had been one of the first to see', Marguerite Fiévez and Jacques Meert wrote. 'But he had serious reservations because he saw immediately a danger here of minimising and even substituting for the proper mission of the laity.'

Nevertheless, unlike French YCW chaplain, Georges Guérin, he did encourage the experience.[45]

Moreover, 'from 1944, the French YCW made enough changes in method and approach to cause some real tension with the Belgian YCW and within the international YCW. Cardijn was worried and preoccupied', Fiévez and Meert say.

---

43. For example Congar, 'Pour une théologie du laïcat', *Etudes* (janv. et fév 1948): 42–54 and 194–218. Cited in Bernard Minvielle, *L'apostolat des laïcs à la veille du Concile* (Fribourg: Editions universitaires Fribourg Suisse, 2001), 50. See also Congar, *Sacerdoce et laïcat.*

44. Fiévez-Meert, *Cardijn*, 177.

45. Emile Poulat, *Naissance des prêtres ouvriers* (Paris: Series Religion et sociétes, Casterman, 1965), 511.

These reservations were also shared within the developing International YCW. An English member of the YCW International Bureau, Kevin Muir, recalled that 'there was some anxiety about the direction that the French Church was taking'.[46] Thus, it is not a surprise that there would also be questions from the Holy See.

As usual, Cardijn decided to tackle these problems head on. In October 1949, he organised a four-day meeting of YCW chaplains from France, England and Belgium with a a group of theologians and specialists, including from France the Dominicans Chenu and Congar, the sociologist Henri Desroches as well as the Belgians Albert Dondeyne, Gustave Thils and Roger Aubert.

'Discussions ranged over the whole field of the spiritual and the temporal in the light of new theological insights and pastoral experiences but for Cardijn the point at issue was the future orientation of the YCW', Fiévez and Meert report. 'The session helped to clear the air but more time and experience would be needed to resolve the differences.'[47]

There is no indication of the positions taken by Congar at this meeting but it would remain the only occasion that Congar worked closely with Cardijn until Vatican II.[48]

Exile and international prominence

Two years later the first International Congress of the Lay Apostolate took place in Rome from 7–14 October 1951. Initially Cardijn feared that the congress would be dominated by Italian style Catholic Action. After meeting the organising committee, however, he changed his views and gave his strong backing to the congress, eventually delivering a powerful keynote speech that confirmed Cardijn's pre-eminence as an international authority on lay apostolate issues.[49]

---

46. Kevin Muir, *The international character of the YCW: A cause of controversy* in *First Steps towards a history of the IYCW* (Brussels: International Cardijn Foundation, 2000), 132.

47. Fiévez-Meert, *Cardijn*, 166.

48. Cardijn and Congar did meet on other occasions, however, as documented by Congar in his *Journal d'un théologien* (Paris: Cerf, 2000), 84 and 105.

49. Cardijn, *Discours au Congrès mondial de l'apostolat des laïcs*, October 1951: http://www.josephcardijn.fr/the-apostolate-of-the-laity (Accessed 12/03/2019)

This congress took place only a few weeks before Congar completed his *Jalons pour une théologie du laïcat* which was published the following year.[50] Congar took part in the congress after initially declining an invitation from the chief organiser Vittorino Veronese.[51]

A major outcome of the lay apostolate congress was the establishment by Pope Pius XII on 23 January 1952 of the COPECIAL, being the *Comité Permanent des Congrès Internationaux pour l'Apostolat des Laïcs*. Veronese, who became the secretary of this new organisation, was greatly impressed by Congar's book and wanted to invite him to an expert meeting in 1953.

But by this time, the worker priest affair in France was coming to the climax that resulted in their being ordered to withdraw from the workplaces. Congar also was now increasingly suspect in the eyes of the Roman authorities both for his ecumenical work as well as for his newly published writings on the laity. Although his books were not condemned, from February 1952, he was forbidden to re-print or publish new editions of his *Vraie et fausse réforme dans l'Eglise*.[52]

Thus, paradoxically, at the very moment his *Jalons* was making an impact among lay apostolate leaders worldwide, Congar found himself excluded from formally meeting with international lay apostolate leaders, even before the Holy See moved to have him relocated from Paris resulting in his appointment to Jerusalem in 1954! A year later, he was "exiled" to Cambridge and at the end of 1956 he was moved again to Strasbourg.

Nevertheless, even in the darkest hours, he continued to give talks to various lay groups. The English YCW, for example, took advantage of his exile at Cambridge to invite Congar to address them on 25 June 1956.[53] And as soon as he arrived in Strasbourg, the invitations began to roll in to address lay apostolate groups. But these were smaller lower profile meetings that evidently raised fewer concerns in Rome.

Meanwhile, Australian-born publisher Geoffrey Chapman was preparing the publication of an English translation of *Jalons* under the

---

50. Congar, *Jalons pour une théologie du laïcat* (Paris, Unam Sanctam Series 23, Cerf, 1952). Congar's introduction to the book is dated 22 December 1951.

51. *L'apostolat des laïcs à la veille du Concile*, 115.

52. François LePrieur, *Quand Rome condamne* (Paris: Terre Humaine Series, Plon/ Cerf, 1989), 26.

53. Congar, *Liste de prédications*. Congar Archives.

title of *Lay People in the* Church,[54] the first edition of which appeared in 1957 just in time for the Second International Congress of the Lay Apostolate held in Rome from 5–13 October.

Once again Cardijn and the lay leaders of the YCW played a prominent role at the congress. In fact, only a few weeks earlier, the International YCW had organised an international pilgrimage to Rome for 32,000 young workers, who gathered with Pope Pius XII in St Peter's Square on 25 August 1957. This was followed by the first IYCW International Council.

But Congar was still blacklisted by the Holy See and thus unable to participate at the lay apostolate congress despite his growing international prominence on theology of the laity issues.

Moreover, it is somewhat paradoxical that after Congar's earlier references to Cardijn and the YCW in *Chrétiens Désunis* and *Vraie et fausse réforme*, the only direct reference to the movement in *Jalons*, which is devoted to laity issues, is a relatively minor example of a YCW enquiry on a local French issue.[55] In addition, the English edition of *Jalons* eliminates the reference to the YCW which in fact makes no sense outside the French context without further explanation.

It is also striking that in a thirteen page list of some 1,200 authors cited in *Jalons* Congar fails to make even a single reference to Cardijn. This no doubt says a lot about how Congar viewed Cardijn, e.g. as a prophetic figure but not as a theologian. In any event, the book certainly addresses many themes that were inspired by the experience of Cardijn and the YCW.

At the same time, it may also help explain why later generations of YCW chaplains and leaders failed to identify with Congar's landmark work.

In spite of all this, Congar continued his always punishing schedule of speaking and preaching to church groups and lay movements mostly in France. In 1959, he again addressed a group of YCW and ACO chaplains at Puxe, near Metz. This is certainly one of the last talks specifically given to a group linked to the YCW.[56] More than

---

54. Yves Congar, *Lay People in the Church* (London: Geoffrey Chapman, 1957) (Revised edition 1964).

55. Congar, *Jalons pour une théologie du laïcat*, second edition, Unam Sanctam Series 23 (Paris: Cerf, 1951), 483.

56. There is one more talk on 1 May 1964 that may refer to the YCW (writing difficult to read). And there are other talks given to various Catholic Action groups that probably include YCW leaders and chaplains.

twenty-five years of direct service and involvement with the movement had come to their conclusion.

Cardijn and Congar at Vatican II

Cardijn and the Lay Apostolate Commission

It was Pope John XXIII himself who expressed the wish for the establishment of a Lay Apostolate Commission to prepare Vatican II after Council organisers apparently failed to include such a commission in their early proposals.[57]

Cardijn, who was still the chaplain of the International YCW, was appointed as an expert on this commission which was chaired by Cardinal Fernando Cento,[58] who had previously been nuncio in Brussels, with Mgr Achille Glorieux,[59] a former jocist chaplain from Lille, as secretary. But the theologians 'who had done the most to advance the theology of the laity: Congar, Philips, Rahner, Schillebeeckx, von Balthasar, Chenu' were conspicuously absent from the commission.[60]

Nevertheless, Cardijn worked extremely hard during the Council attending each meeting of the commission as well as each session of the Council. Despite a still heavy schedule and the fact that he celebrated his eightieth birthday a month after the Council opened, his papers show the meticulous way that he read each draft of the planned decree on lay apostolate and the various critiques and notes that he prepared in a bid to improve the various drafts.[61]

It is evident that Cardijn was far from satisfied with the early drafts of the decree. This is hardly surprising given that most of the drafting was done in small sub-commission groups dominated by

---

57. Joseph Komonchak, *The struggle for the Council during the preparation of Vatican II (1960–1962)* in Giuseppe Alberigo, editor (English edition edited by Joseph Komonchak) *History of Vatican II*, Volume I (Maryknoll/Leuven: Orbis/Peeters, 1995), 196–197.

58. Cardinal Fernando Cento (1883–1973), Nuncio in Brussels 1946–1953. http://www.catholic-hierarchy.org/bishop/bcento.html (Accessed 12/03/2019)

59. Msgr later Archbishop Achille Glorieux (1910–1999) http://www.catholic-hierarchy.org/bishop/bglori.html (Accessed 12/03/2019)

60. Msgr later Archbishop Achille Glorieux (1910–1999).

61. Cardijn's personal notes and papers on the Council fill 102 folders of his personal archives. Folders 1529–1630. The archives of the International YCW show the work that he did with the movement concerning the Council.

Italian drafters. Thus, the difference between Italian-style Catholic Action dependent on the hierarchy and the Belgian-French concept defended and developed by Cardijn loomed large in the discussions.[62]

Meanwhile, he also worked hard to involve the International YCW in the preparation of the Council. This included a highly organised plan to lobby Council Fathers in as many countries as possible of the countries where the YCW was present.

In 1963, Cardijn published his only full-length book, *Laïcs en premières lignes*, a compilation and updating of his major articles on the lay apostolate of the previous thirty years, which was also translated into English, Spanish and German.[63]

Congar on the other hand had been appointed to the Theological Preparatory Commission. The result, as Congar later noted, was that he and Cardijn had little contact during the preparation and early sessions of the Council.

'I only saw him in the Mixed Commission (Theology and Laity) preparing Schema XVII which became Schema XIII (*Gaudium et Spes*)', Congar wrote to Marguerite Fiévez.[64] 'But I hardly saw him and I don't remember any notable intervention.'

Cardijn a cardinal

However, Congar was delighted when Pope Paul VI appointed him a cardinal in the consistory of February 1965 meaning that Cardijn would be a Council Father for the Fourth Session later that year. Clearly, he hoped for big things from Cardijn.

'But then he became a cardinal. I hoped that his prestige, that I believed to be immense, would enable him to play an important role

---

62. Komonchak, *The struggle for the Council during the preparation of Vatican II (1960–1962)*, 198–99.
63. The English edition, *Laymen into Action*, was published Geoffrey Chapman, who had previously got his start in publishing with an earlier compilation of Cardijn's articles, *Challenge to Action*. (Joseph Cardijn, *Laymen into Action* (Melbourne: YCW, 1964) and Joseph Cardijn, *Challenge to Action* (Melbourne: YCW, 1955)).
64. « Au Concile, Mgr Cardijn travaillait à la Commission de l'Apostolat des Laïcs dans laquelle je n'ai pas travaillé. Je ne l'ai vu que dans la Commission mixte (Théologie et Laïcs) préparant le Schema XVII devenu le Schema XIII (Gaudium et Spes). Mais je n'ai guère vu et n'ai pas le souvenir d'intervention notable. » Congar, *Letter to Marguerite Fiévez*, 22 October 1975. http://priests.josephcardijn.com/testimony-on-cardijn

in the 4th period of the Council (1965)', Congar noted in his Council Journal.[65]

The fact that Cardijn had chosen a worker parish as his titular parish also impressed Congar.

'This means that the issue of simplifying the vestments of a cardinal is now on the table. For sure, silk will be abandoned. Phew!' he noted.

But he was not impressed by the ceremony at which Cardijn received his biglietto.

'Arrived at Propaganda at 9.30', Congar wrote. 'The tickets only arrived at 10.40. Reading of the double announcement to Archbishop Cooray, Martin, Villot, Zoungrana, Duval, Cardijn. I came mostly for Cardijn, Journet and Duval. Each double announcement was read six times, followed by Cooray's speech, then Martin's (three times longer than it should be) . . . We returned at 1.20pm. Five hours wasted . . . I came out morally crushed.'

The saving grace was that he was able to meet Cardijn.

'I greeted the cardinals but Cardijn most of all', Congar's notes continued. 'He embraced everyone and tapped them on the back, a bit like Father Chenu. He is the most authentic (with Seper) of all the ones I saw. He said: 'They have given me the opportunity to speak. I hope to use it as well as possible!''

'His ordination yesterday was magnificent, it seems, with 800 jocists from Belgium singing and praying. He said to me: "Help me! Keep helping me! I will need it. We must continue to move forward!"'

A weekend in Switzerland with Congar

Soon after his cardinalate, however, Cardijn was on the road again on a four-month voyage to Asia and Australia and unable to do much preparation for the Council.

By the time he returned to Brussels, time was running short. In July, he wrote to Council secretary-general Cardinal Pericle Felici requesting copies of the draft documents to be discussed in the final

---

65. « Puis il devint cardinal. J'espérais que son prestige, que je croyais immense, lui permettrai de jouer un rôle important dans le 4ème période du Concile (1965). » Congar, *Letter to Marguerite Fiévez*,

session, none of which had evidently been sent to him previously but Felici replied that they were still being printed.[66]

Meanwhile, Congar, took the initiative to write to Cardijn on 11 July 1965.[67]

'You said to me at the time of your cardinalate: "They have given me the chance to speak, I will make use of it", Congar wrote.

> The 4th session will begin soon, and those who wish to speak on religious freedom must send their summary before 9 September. We can expect that there will be many critiques, perhaps quite ferocious. Moreover, there will also need to be a '*Laus Declarationis*'[68]—without, evidently, hiding whatever may be considered to be inadequate and thus capable of being improved. I said to myself, in my candour, that you would be very closely listened to if, in the name of your worldwide experience, you said what positive outcomes we can expect from the Declaration, if necessary by responding to the critiques which will certainly be made and which, in effect, come to mind, such as favouring the propagation of error.

'Certainly, you will also speak on Schema XIII. I therefore ask if, in the presentation of the meaning of the world with respect to Christ and to eschatology, and also in the chapter on culture, enough place has been given to workers and to the immense enterprise of Production by the hands and mind of man.'

'I therefore suggest these things in the spirit in which you wrote and said at your cardinalate: "I am counting on you".'[69]

Cardijn wrote back immediately seeking a meeting.

---

66. Cardijn, Letter to Cardinal Felici, 19 July 1965. Cardijn Archives 1575.
67. Cardijn had just returned from a four month trip to Asia including Australia. Fiévez-Meert, 192.
68. Declaration of praise.
69. « Bien certainement, vous parlerez aussi sur le schéma XIII. Je me demande si, dans la présentation du sens du monde par rapport au Christ et à l'eschatologie, et aussi dans le chapitre sur la culture, on a fait une place suffisante aux ouvriers, à l'immense entreprise de la Production par les bras et l'esprit de l'homme. Je vous suggère ces choses dans l'esprit de simplicité avec lequel vous m'avez écrit et dit, lors de votre cardinalat : « Je compte sur vous ». » Congar, Letter to Cardijn, 11 July 1965. This letter thus appears to be responding to an earlier letter from Cardijn. But there is no copy of any earlier letter in the Cardijn Archives in Brussels. The original may be in the Congar Archives.

'I have not yet had time to study the Council Schemas!' he wrote back to Congar. 'I am running more than ever. I still need to prepare the World Council of the YCW in Bangkok in November–December. I am overwhelmed.'

> I will read the Schema on Religious Freedom and send you my reactions. It is my practice to look at problems from the point of view of people whereas theoreticians look at them from the point of view of principles. The doctors say: 'Man is free' whereas I say 'Three quarters of men are not free; we need to liberate them.' This is the problem of young people and adults in the world today, both in developed and underdeveloped countries. What a problem! If we could only come to an agreement on how to tackle the problem, what unity, what collaboration, what peace we could build![70]

And so Cardijn proposed to meet with Congar either at Strasbourg 'unless you can meet me half way in Luxembourg'.

Eight days later, Congar replied saying that 'the problem of the necessity of liberating men is of a very real and urgency and density but that this will be an issue for Schema XIII.'

'The Declaration on Religious Freedom is limited to the juridical level. That is its limit but also its strength, and that is why in my opinion it will get support from 95% of the Council Fathers.'[71]

---

70. « Je n'ai pas encore eu le temps d'étudier les Schémas du Concile ! Je cours plus que jamais. La semaine prochaine encore à Lourdes. Il me faut encore préparer le Conseil Mondial de la JOC à Bangkok, de novembre à décembre. Je suis débordé. J'espère que le Saint Esprit m'éclairera et me soutiendra. Vous, soyez un peu mon guide dans une matière où je ne suis qu'un novice. Je vais lire le Schéma sur la Liberté Religieuse et vous enverrai nos réactions. Je suis habitué à voir les problèmes du côté des hommes et les théoriciens du côté des principes. Les docteurs disent : « L'homme est libre » ; et moi je dis : « Les trois quarts des hommes ne sont pas libres ; il faut les libérer » . C'est le problème des jeunes comme des adultes dans le monde d'aujourd'hui, dans les pays développés comme dans les pays sous-développés. Quel problème ! Si on pouvait s'entendre sur la façon de poser le problème, quelle unité, quelle collaboration, quelle paix on parviendrait à susciter ! » Cardijn, *Letter to Congar*, 14 July 1965. Cardijn Archives 1579.

71. « Le problème de la nécessité de libérer les hommes est d'une densité, d'une urgence bien réelles, mais ce serait plutôt un problème pour le Schema XIII. La Déclaration sur la liberté religieuse se tient au plan juridique. C'est sa limite, mais c'est sa force, et ce que fait qu'à mon avis, elle doit rallier 95 % des Pères Conciliaires. » Congar, Letter to Cardijn, *22 July 1965*. Cardijn Archives 1579.

But Congar was going to Geneva for a meeting at Bossey with the World Council of Churches. This did not deter Cardijn and after a flurry of phone calls, aged eighty-two, he took a plane to Geneva to meet Congar and his old colleague Fr Henri Féret.

Congar relates the story in his Council Journal:

> The great moment from the point of view of the Council was the arrival of Cardinal Cardijn . . . He arrived on 4 August at 12.40pm at the Geneva airport. We began to talk immediately in the car. It was an extraordinary Feast of St Dominic for us, two grace-filled half days. I think it was not in vain that this (opportunity) was given to me.
>
> Concerning Rome, the pope's projects, the reform of the Curia, the progress of the Council, Cardijn says he knows nothing, and in fact I believe that he knows little or nothing. He told me that since his cardinalate he had not received a single paper even once telling him what is expected of him. Since he was named to the Congregation for Studies and Seminaries, he went to see Pizzardo. He left completely bewildered. Pizzardo is a nothing.
>
> He told me about his cardinalate, how the Pope told him to 'remain Cardijn'!. Cardijn is very free![72]

---

72. « . . . Mais le grand moment, au point de vue travail conciliaire, a été la venue du cardinal Cardijn. Il m'avait écrit avec insistance qu'il voulait me voir. Le 1er août, je lui ai téléphoné à Bruxelles. Il est arrivé le 4 août à 12 h 40 à l'aérodrome de Genève. Tout de suite, puis en voiture, on a parlé. Ce fut pour nous une extraordinaire Saint-Dominique, deux demi-journées de grâce. Je crois que ce n'est pas en vain que cela m'a été donné. Sur Rome, sur les projets du pape, la Réforme de la Curie, la marche du concile, Cardijn dit ne rien savoir, et je crois qu'effectivement il ne sait à peu près rien. Il dit n'avoir pas reçu une seule fois un papier depuis son cardinalat, le renseignant sur ce qu'on attendrait de lui. Appartenant à la Congrégation des Études et Séminaires, il est allé voir Pizzardo. Il en est sorti effaré. Pizzardo est un néant, dit-il. Il nous parle de son cardinalat, comment le nonce le lui a annoncé, comment le Pape lui a dit : « Restez Cardijn ! » ; comment, depuis sa pourpre, tout le monde, à Rome, lui sourit, lui fait courbettes (« c'est dégoûtant », dit-il, « c'est ignoble. Je n'aurais jamais cru cela »). Cardijn est très libre ; il reste tout à fait lui-même. Et quel entrain, quel enthousiasme ; quelle santé chez cet homme de quatre-vingt-trois ans ! » Yves Congar, *My journal of the Council* (Adelaide: ATF Press, 2012), 769 and Yves Congar *Mon journal du Concile* (Presented et annotated by Eric Mahieu), Volume II (Paris: Cerf, 2002), 382–383.

'We talked about religious freedom, Schema XIII, the apostolate of the laity, the missions, priests. Cardijn had prepared reactions on these texts. He counted on me, on us, to test them and put them in the form of Council interventions.'

'Ultimately Cardijn has only one idea but it is consubstantial with him. He is absolutely faithful to it as he is faithful to himself. It throws light on everything. His great idea is to start from the real, the concrete. It is necessary to take people as they are.'

'He criticised the new schema on the apostolate of the laity for beginning by distinguishing kinds of apostolate, for proposing a "spirituality of lay people". If I had started like that, he said, I would never have done anything. I have never met anyone to whom such schemes apply. It is always necessary to begin by taking people as they are, without trying to place them into our frameworks, our ideas, our requirements. It is necessary that it comes from them, it has to be authentic for them. When one starts from a system, one easily forms the idea that nothing can be done with these or those people. So one does nothing', Congar quoted Cardijn as saying.

Cardijn told Congar of his own experience in the parish of Laeken.

'There was a whole neighbourhood of poor people where neither the parish or curate had ever visited. "Nothing can be done!" And Cardijn expressed his intention to go. "They will not welcome you." So the next day Cardijn began to visit. They opened their doors, he drank their coffee. A year later he had a group of a thousand women in that neighbourhood! And he made analogous criticisms of Schema XIII, the Schema on the Missions.'[73]

---

73. « On parle de la Liberté religieuse, du schéma XIII, de l'Apostolat des laïcs, des Missions, des Prêtres. Cardijn a préparé des réactions sur ces textes ; il compte sur moi, sur nous, pour les éprouver et les mettre en forme d'interventions conciliaires. Au fond, Cardijn n'a qu'une idée, mais elle lui est consubstantielle, il lui est absolument fidèle comme il est fidèle à soi-même. Elle éclaire tout. Sa grande idée est de partir du réel, du concret. Il faut prendre les hommes tels qu'ils sont. Il reproche au nouveau schéma sur l'apostolat des laïcs de commencer par distinguer des espèces de l'apostolat, de proposer une « spiritualité des laïcs ». Si j'avais commencé ainsi, dit-il, je n'aurais rien fait. Je n'ai pas rencontré de gens à qui ces schèmes puissent s'appliquer. Il faut toujours commencer par prendre les hommes tels qu'ils sont, sans vouloir plaquer sur eux nos cadres, nos idées, nos exigences. Il faut que cela vienne d'eux, il faut que ce soit authentique pour eux. Quand on part d'un système, on se forme facilement l'idée qu'avec tels ou tels hommes il n'y a rien à faire. Et l'on ne fait rien. Cardijn enseignait dans un

"Little by little we determined a certain number of interventions to make based on his notes and our conversation," Congar noted.

Preparing the speeches

The real work for Congar and Féret began after the weekend with Cardijn.

'Following his departure the next day, Fr Féret and I shared out the work. On the 10th, I sent him a draft of an intervention on religious freedom', Congar's notes record.[74]

'It is a transcription in poor Latin of your draft, shortened by the two pages that referred more to freedom from the interior and moral point of view. We might have been able to make a short point where we ask that the last few lines in the conclusion of the Schema speak of the pastoral duty to educate people in true liberty be somewhat amplified', he wrote in his letter enclosing the draft.[75]

'It's only a draft. I worked on it without a dictionary', Congar continued. 'Fr Féret will send you a draft tomorrow of the text on Schema XIII. It's very hard hitting.'

---

séminaire ou une école quand le cardinal Mercier l'a nommé vicaire à Laeken. Il fut mal accueilli par son curé-doyen qui projeta d'emblée sur lui les étiquettes : pas de santé, ne parle pas flamand, vient d'un séminaire et ne connaît rien ! Or il y avait un quartier de gens pauvres où ni le doyen ni aucun prêtre n'était jamais allé : « Il n'y a rien à faire ! » Et comme Cardijn exprimait son intention d'y aller : « Ils ne vous recevront pas. » Or Cardijn y alla dès le lendemain, on lui ouvrit, il but le café : un an après, il avait un groupe de mille femmes catholiques de ce quartier ! » Congar, *Journal of the Council*, 770 and Congar, *Mon journal du Concile*, Vol. II, 383.

74. « Il fait des critiques analogues au schéma XIII, au schéma sur les Missions. Petit à petit, nous déterminons un certain nombre d'interventions à faire, à partir de ses notes et de notre conversation. Après le départ du cardinal, que nous reconduisons le 5 à son avion de 13 h 40, nous nous distribuons le travail, le P. Féret et moi. Le 10, je lui envoie un projet d'intervention sur la Liberté religieuse. » Congar, *Journal of the Council*, 770 and Congar, *Mon journal du Concile*, Vol. II, 383.

75. « Voici une esquisse de texte d'une intervention sur la Liberté religieuse. C'est une transcription, en un mauvais latin, de votre propre projet, allégé de 2 pages qui parlaient de la liberté plutôt au point de vue intérieure et moral. On aurait pu faire un point assez bref où l'on aurait demandé que les quelques lignes qui, dans la conclusion du Schéma, parlent du devoir pastoral d'éduquer des hommes de vraie liberté, soient quelque peu amplifiées. » Congar, *Letter to Cardijn*, 10 August 1965. Cardijn Archives 1579.

'Your visit was a great grace for me, for both of us . . . I will send more drafts on the Missions and the Priesthood from Strasbourg. They are not so urgent', Congar concluded.[76]

Cardijn's Archives in Brussels contain the copies of these texts, which ultimately morphed into the three speeches that Cardijn delivered *in aula* at the Council, one on religious liberty and two on Schema XIII. Also in the archives are two more speeches on the lay apostolate and on the ministry of the priest, neither of which were delivered orally but which were presumably submitted to the Council secretariat. However, there is no record of any speech on Missions.

By 20 August, the various draft speeches were all ready and sent to the Council secretariat.

On 14 September, Cardijn sought a meeting in Rome with Congar and Féret to put the final touches to his preparations.

Again Congar noted that Cardijn was out of the loop.

'He knows nothing, sees no-one, is not involved in anything. But his interventions are ready and he is ready to give a few good fist blows', Congar wrote in his notes.[77]

Indeed, the five speeches are classic Cardijn speeches combining deceptively simple and homely references based on his own experiences with his own theological insights and encapsulating the core of Cardijn's message.

---

76. « Ce n'est qu'un projet. J'ai travaillé sans aucun dictionnaire. Si vous voulez faire vos remarques, supprimer, ajouter, je pourrai le faire facilement à Strasbourg, où je rentre dans la nuit du 13 au 14. Je pars d'ici, dans un instant (aérodrome Genève) pour donner deux conférences à la Semaine missiologique de Burgos. Le P. Féret vous enverra demain un projet de texte sur le Schéma XIII, conformément à votre papier, vos instructions et notre conversation. Il me l'a lu en brouillon : c'est vigoureux. Nous gardons un souvenir bénir de votre passage ici. Ce fut pour moi, pour nous, une grande grâce. Je vous remercie une nouvelle fois de vous être imposé ce voyage. Du reste, je vous enverrai, de Strasbourg, d'autres projets, rédigés d'après vos indications, sur les Missions et les prêtres. Mais cela presse moins puisque la discussion sur ces points ne viendra qu'en fin de sept. ou début octobre. » *Ibid.*

77. « 14 sept 1965 : Féret m'avait dit hier que Cardijn nous demandait devenir déjeuner après la cérémonie de ce matin. Je n'ai aucune précision [finalement, je vois rue Ulisse Seni . . . il y a eu mal donne . . . Retard du P. Féret.]. Il y a beau jeu qu'on a achevé de déjeuner et que le cardinal, fatigue, est allé faire une sieste. Quand il revient, on travaille un peu en prenant le café, dans le jardin. Il ne sait rien, ne voit personne, n'est mêlé à rien. Mais ses interventions sont prêtes, et il est disposé à donner quelques bons coups de poing . . . » Congar, *Mon journal du Concile*, Volume II, 389 and Congar, *My Council Journal*, 775.

The specific and irreplaceable lay apostolate of lay people

It is a pity that Cardijn did not have the opportunity to deliver his speeches on lay apostolate and priestly ministry because taken together they offer an elegant summary of his vision of the partnership that should exist between the priesthood of the faithful and the ministerial priesthood. It is equally clear that Congar has fully grasped Cardijn's vision and formulated it beautifully in the draft speeches.

'During the sixty years I have lived with young workers', Cardijn stated in his never delivered speech on lay apostolate, 'I never met any who are immediately concerned with spirituality and moved by supernatural ends'.

'But from the beginning I took an interest in their work and their lives. I asked what they were thinking, what they thought about their work, their housing, their recreation and all the various aspects of their lives. We started to become friends. We searched together how to improve, to help others. We met together as militants to do this review of life. Together we made recollections and retreats . . . Little by little they began to understand the need for the sacraments, the mass and communion to unite themselves with Christ, to live with Him, by Him.'

'We cannot transform the world without them. THEY are the Church in the world of today, together with their families, as well as their influence in all the key posts of national and international life but most of all **at the grassroots, in ordinary and daily** life', Cardijn says.

This implied the 'absolute necessity and irreplaceable importance of the apostolate of lay people'.

But in order to form such lay apostles, Cardijn insisted, 'we must first of all be convinced of this fundamental truth, namely that the apostolate of lay people is the lay life of lay people" from local to international level, as well the 'divine value" of that life and the 'transformation that must take place with, by and in Christ and the Church, with the resources of the Church (prayer, sacraments, etc.) but which are incarnated in the affairs of the world.'

Vatican II did accept this vision of the lay apostolate, although undoubtedly in less elegant and less forceful terms than Cardijn's own. *Lumen Gentium* recognised the 'special' role of lay people in making the Church 'present and operative in those places and circumstances where only through them can it become the salt of the earth'[78] while *Apostolicam Actuositatem* opens with a reference to the 'proper and indispensable role' of lay people.[79]

Priests serving the lay apostolate

Cardijn's undelivered speech on priestly ministry provides the corollary to his emphasis on lay apostolate. Again he insists on the need for priests to reach out to lay people.

'"he starting point is listening to people and striving to understand, to love them and and accept them as they are', Cardijn says.

And the way in which this is done is vital.

'When they come to us asking for the sacraments or other things of that nature, they will be open to us or not depending on the sincerity of our humanity. If ultimately they come! Many of them would have never even come in contact with the church or a man of the church!'

Therefore, the Church 'must leave its confines and meet the people wherever they really are'.

'This was also the conclusion of Cardinal Suhard of happy memory', Cardijn continued in reference to the Paris archbishop who had been so moved by Godin and Daniel's book.

But priests will not succeed in engaging with people if they are lacking in faith and fidelity, Cardijn warns. 'We must insist on this', he says. It is the only way to overcome the isolation of people and eventually form a community, a missionary community.

Religious freedom

Cardijn did succeed in delivering his speech on religious freedom to the Council Fathers on 23 September 1965.

It is significant to note that Cardijn, meticulous as always, also submitted his draft paper to his long-standing colleague, the philosopher Fr Albert Dondeyne, as well as to his friend Bishop Emile-

---

78. 'Now the laity are called in a special way to make the Church present and operative in those places and circumstances where only through them can it become the salt of the earth', *Lumen Gentium*, §33.

79. *Apostolicam Actuositatem*, §1.

Joseph De Smedt,[80] who chaired the commission responsible for the declaration on religious freedom.

As Congar had proposed, Cardijn the talk begins by emphasising the need to proclaim the juridical dimension of religious freedom.[81] In support of this, he cites what we would perhaps today refer to as the increasing globalisation of the world.

'As John XXIII stated so admirably in *Pacem in Terris*, our great task is to unite ourselves with all men of good will to build a more human world together based on 'truth, justice, liberty and love'. And the fundamental condition for people to live together peacefully and to collaborate fruitfully is sincere respect for religious freedom', Cardijn argues.

Indeed, failing to respect the convictions of others 'makes mutual confidence impossible' and 'without this there can be no true community life' or collaboration, he warns. Hence, 'the presence of the Church among the people must necessarily take a new form, which could be compared to the dispersion of the people of Israel after the captivity of Babylon'.

'In most parts of the world', Cardijn notes, 'Christians are a small minority'. It is not possible (or desirable, Cardijn implied) for the Church 'to base itself on temporal, political, economic or cultural power as it did in the Middle Ages or under colonial regimes'.

On the contrary, the Church 'can rely only on the power of the word of God, evangelical poverty, the purity of its witness, manifested in the authentically Christian life of lay people, and also on the esteem of the peoples among whom the Church wishes to live and witness to its faith'.

But the ultimate reason for proclaiming religious freedom, Cardijn says, is its educational value. 'It is a necessary means for education in

---

80. Bishop De Smedt was a friend of Cardijn of long standing. His sister, Livine De Smedt, had been a fulltime worker for the YCW in the Diocese of Bruges. Retired Bruges vicar-general Father Leo De Clerck confirmed to me the links between Cardijn and De Smedt. Bishop De Smedt's archives also contain correspondence with Cardijn relating to the drafting of his pastoral letter on the priesthood of the faithful published in 1961 and which had a great impact at the Council. *Cf* E-J De Smedt, *Le sacerdoce des fidèles* (Bruges/Paris: Desclée de Brouwer, 1961). English edition: E-J De Smedt, *The Priesthood of the Faithful* (New York: Deus Books/Paulist Press, 1962).
81. The various drafts can be found in the Cardijn Archives.

liberty in its fullest sense, which leads to interior freedom, or freedom of the soul by which a man becomes an autonomous being, responsible before society and God.'

'This interior freedom, even if it exists in germ as a natural gift in every human creature, requires a long education which can be summarised in three words: see, judge and act', Cardijn argues.

Instead of trying to shelter people from the dangers of life, 'I showed confidence in their freedom in order to better educate that freedom', he continues.

'I helped them to see, judge and act by themselves, by undertaking social and cultural action themselves, freely obeying authorities in order to become adult witnesses of Christ and the Gospel, conscious of being responsible for their sisters and brothers in the whole world.'

For Cardijn then, the see-judge-act method is the necessary corollary of religious freedom. The more people are free, the more they need to be educated in that freedom, the more they need to develop a consciousness of their responsibilities, he says.

It is a powerful argument and sums up Cardijn's whole educational philosophy. However, according to Congar, the speech failed to make an impact on the audience.

'Cardinal Cardijn spoke a little like a tribune. People were sympathetic, but it did not work. It had no impact and people were gently critical concerning his style', Congar related.[82]

Nevertheless, although his speech may not have made the hoped for impact *in aula*, it is striking to read the final version of the Declaration on Religious Freedom adopted by the Council. The opening lines of *Dignitatis Humanae* could have virtually been lifted from his speech:

'A sense of the dignity of the human person has been impressing itself more and more deeply on the consciousness of contemporary man, and the demand is increasingly made that men should act on their own judgment, enjoying and making use of a responsible freedom, not driven by coercion but motivated by a sense of duty.'[83]

---

82. « Le cardinal Cardijn parle, un peu en tribun. On lui garde sympathie, mais cela ne passe pas. Cela n'a aucune influence et l'on est gentiment critique sur le genre. » Congar, *Mon journal du Concile*, Volume II, 404 and Congar, *My Journal of the Council*, 786.

83. Here the word 'duty' in English translates the Latin word *officii* which elsewhere in Vatican II documents is translated as 'responsibility'.

Moreover, Paragraph 8 urges those 'charged with the task of educating others to do their utmost to form men . . . who will come to decisions on their own judgement and in the light of truth, govern their activities with a sense of responsibility, and strive after what is true and right, willing always to join with others in cooperative effort.'

This is a clear endorsement of Cardijn's see-judge-act method in this context of striving for a greater sense or consciousness of people's responsibilities. In fact, the method had already gained recognition in Pope John's encyclical *Mater et* Magistra.[84] And *Apostolicam Actuositatem* again canonised the method[85] and indeed the method which was also followed in the drafting and organisation of *Gaudium et Spes* itself.[86]

Cardijn's hard-hitting speeches on Schema XIII

As noted by Congar, Fr Féret drafted Cardijn's 'hard-hitting' second and third speeches on Schema XIII, which was to become *Gaudium et Spes*. In effect, it is one speech divided into two parts to fit in to the time limits imposed by the procedural rules of the Council.

Cardijn delivered the speeches on 23 September and 5 October. Cardinal Suenens of Brussels was chairing but Cardijn failed to hear

---

84. Pope John XXIII, *Mater et magistra*, §236.
85. *Apostolicam Actuositatem.*
86. 'The change in methodology was monumental: it represented a shift from a perspective that was dogmatic, deductive and top-to-bottom to one that was exploratory, inductive, and bottom-to-top. If nothing more than this structural change had been made, a giant step would have been taken. In fact, much more than advancement than just methodological would be achieved . . . Many theologians now believe that the methodology of Gaudium et Spes is every bit as important as its content. The methodology used in the document turns traditional theology on its head. Instead of proceeding in the time-honored fashion, discussing theological or biblical principles and then applying them to a present-day situation, Gaudium et Spes reverses the process: it begins with a careful analysis of the de facto situation, then turns to sacred scripture and theology for reflection on that situation, and finally, as a third step, makes pastoral applications. Theological reflection thus becomes the second, not the first, step.' Edward Cleary O.P. *Crisis and Change: The Church in Latin America Today* (New York: Orbis Books, 1985), Chapter 2 and 3. Cited in Stephanie Block, *Liberationism and Liberationist Materials Used by Catholics in the United States*, Dossier http://www.catholicmediacoalition.org/USCCB%20Dossier%20on%20 Liberationism.doc

the warning bell and went overtime, evidently alienating many in his audience.[87]

Content-wise, however, they are classic Cardijn speeches. He begins by emphasising the significant demographic position of young people.

'This is why, by this constitution, the Council must address a special message to young people today in which it will express its confidence and encourage them in their respective milieux to become conscious of their responsibilities with respect to our era and that of tomorrow.'

But 'rather than addressing young people with paternal exhortations, the Council must give them a virile consciousness of their responsibilities', Cardijn insisted.

He condemns the 'great international justice' of underdevelopment in the Third World nations.

'It will certainly cause a historic scandal if the present state of affairs were to continue whereby "Christian" countries maintain the possession and use of the greater part of the riches of the world', Cardijn warns.

He amplifies this in the second speech on 5 October, condemning 'the sub-human situation of the majority of the working world'.

'The majority of or even the great majority of workers presently experience deplorable and gravely unjust working conditions, including derisory wages, unemployment, inadequate housing, etc.

'Whatever is contrary to Catholic Social Teaching must be considered as gravely sinful', Cardijn told the Council Fathers.

Work must 'no longer serve to produce arms which destroy houses and kill children but to build houses, to provide food for children and to better instruct and train young people.'

But most of all, 'the Church which loves the workers as Our Lord Jesus Christ loved them must be convinced that workers are and must be their own liberators', Cardijn said.

---

87. 'The day when he spoke on youth, and the developing countries, Cardinal Suenens was presiding. Cardijn was rather scared at having to give his long text in Latin but he went ahead with all the force and stress with which he was accustomed to address large gatherings. Indeed he was quite carried away by his subject and his convictions, failed to notice that his time was up and failed, too, to hear the President trying to halt him with the tap of his hammer. He went on with even more fire!' Fiévez – Meert, *Cardijn*, 226.

Cardijn also made a number of specific proposals.

'This is why I greatly desire', he said on 23 September, 'that the introduction to the first part of the document should be entitled "the human condition in the world today." Indeed this is precisely the title found in the Latin version *"De hominis condicione in mundo hodierno."*

He also requested 'that there be added three sections, or alternatively one section with three paragraphs, to be devoted respectively to young people, to workers and to the peoples of the Third World.'

'These sections or paragraphs would give a concrete and dynamic character to the whole introduction', he said. But he was not successful in this request.

Similarly, the Council did not retain Cardijn's request for 'a solemn invitation to all world authorities, religious or political, private or public, national or international to renounce their present conflicts and to effectively and without delay set out to coordinate all the immense opportunities present in the world created by God as well as by the efforts of people for the liberation of young people, workers and the Third World.'

Nevertheless, much of the content of Cardijn's request is contained in *Gaudium et Spes*. Moreover, the closing messages of the Council did invite world rulers to be 'the promoters of order and peace among men'.[88]

Congar's evaluation

Immediately following Cardijn's talks, Congar was somewhat disappointed with his impact.

'A very boring discussion on Schema XIII', he wrote on 5 October 1965. 'Cardijn spoke, but less like a tribune than the first time. Contrary to what I had thought, people attach little credit to him ... The cardinal's "orator of the masses" style did not have the impact that I had hoped for. It was not his role and his charism was quite different', Congar concluded.[89]

---

88. Second Vatican Council Closing speeches and messages. http://www.ewtn.com/library/papaldoc/p6closin.htm (Accessed 12/03/2019)

89. « Discussion fort ennuyeux sur le schéma XIII. Cardijn parle, moins en tribun que la première fois. Contrairement à ce que j'avais pensé, on lui attache peu de

Here it is important to remember that the adoption of Schema XIII was still far from certain at that point. Congar evidently hoped that Cardijn would win over the remaining doubters among the bishops with a speech like his memorable 1933 *Ite Missa Est* speech or his earlier 'baptism of the YCW' speech also at Reims in 1927 which moved the archbishop of Paris to tears.[90] This is no doubt a fair evaluation of the immediate impact of Cardijn's speeches. And yet, the evidence is clear of Cardijn's impact on the Council as a whole.

As Fiévez and Meert concluded, 'the Church owes it in large measure to the YCW and so to Cardijn that her theology has been enriched by a new understanding of the laity, ratified and adopted by the Council' in *Lumen Gentium*.[91] The particular contribution of Cardijn and the YCW, they conclude 'was to bring to light the theological import of certain neglected human values, such as the theology of work . . . and also what has been called the theology of secular realities. It was from this kind of ferment that there came the pastoral constitution *Gaudium et Spes*.'

Moreover, writing to Marguerite Fiévez in 1975 ten years after the Council, Congar upheld his earlier view of Cardijn's achievement as the 'perfect example of the assumption at the summit (of the Church) of an initiative coming from the base of the Church'.[92]

Conclusion

However, perhaps it was South African Archbishop Denis Hurley OMI who best appreciated Cardijn's role at the Council, including his impact on Congar and Chenu.

'See, judge and act. That simple formula was a discovery of genius, one of the greatest geniuses who ever pushed along Christian edu-

---

crédit. Je sors un peu. Le cardinal me dit qu'il ne parlera pas sur le sacerdoce . . . C'est un fait qu'en Concile, le genre « orateur de masse » du cardinal n'a pas eu l'écho que j'espérais. Ce n'était pas son métier, et son charisme était autre . . . »

90. Joseph Cardijn, *Interview with BRTN Television*, 1962. http://www.josephcardijn. fr/1962-entretien-television-brtn

91. Fiévez – Meert, *Cardijn*, 228.

92. « La rencontre de son inspiration et de ses premières réalisations avec l'idée de Pie XI sur l'Action Catholique m'apparaissait comme l'exemple parfait de l'assomption au sommet d'une inspiration d'en bas, la synthèse des deux. » Congar, *Letter to Marguerite Fiévez*, 22 October 1975.

cation: Joseph Cardijn. So he founded his Young Christian Workers for the young industrial workers but his method was taken up in all forms of Catholic Action . . .

'But the amazing thing is the effect it had on theologians and first of all the French theologians', Hurley continued, 'especially two very prominent men: Yves Congar and Marie-Dominique Chenu'.

'These theologians, struck by the experiences of the YCW . . . began to revise all their theology and that caused enormous disturbance, upset and unrest in the Catholic Church in France just before, during and just after the Second World War.

'It is amazing the effect the Young Christian Workers had on these theologians and how through their work the whole Catholic Church was revolutionised', Hurley concluded.[93] In essence, this sums up the thirty-year partnership that united Joseph Cardijn and Yves Congar.

Indeed, it is a paradigm example of the influence and impact of Joseph Cardijn on a whole generation of theologians who knew and worked with him, including Fr Chenu, Albert Dondeyne, Gerard Philips, Gustave Thils and others who came to prominence at Vatican II.

---

93. Social Justice: Church & Politics (1986) Archbishop Denis E Hurley, OMI, *St. Joseph's Parish, Greyville* (1986).

InterfaceTheology 3/1 2017

Christifideles Sine Additio or Indoles Saecularis: Yves Congar's Description of the Laity in Dialogue with Contemporary Trends

Christian Raab, OSB

Early in his pontificate Pope Francis stated that the good shepherd of today must leave behind *not* the 99 to fetch the 1, *but* the 1 to fetch the 99.[1] The Holy Father has been lately calling upon the laity to be his partner in this mission, and emphasising the laity's irreplaceable role in ecclesial outreach to the post-Christian secular world, of bringing mercy to the front lines and meeting people where they are. For example, he remarked last November that the duty of the laity was 'to animate every environment, every activity, every human relation according to the Spirit of the Gospel, bringing light, hope, and the charity received from Christ to those places that otherwise would remain foreign to God's action and abandoned to the misery of the human condition'. 'No one better than [the laity]', he said, 'can carry out the essential task of inscribing divine law in the life of the earthly city'.[2]

English columnist, and co-founder of Catholic Voices, Jack Valero has detected in many of Francis's recent remarks an attempt to revive the teaching of *Lumen gentium* that the laity have a "secular character," of *Apostolicam actuositatem* that the lay state is characterized by being a "life led in the midst of the world," and of *Gaudium et Spes*

---

1. See 'Address of Pope Francis to Participants in the Ecclesial Convention of the Diocese of Rome', June 17, 2013, Vatican Website http://w2.vatican.va/content/francesco/en/speeches/2013/june/documents/papa-francesco_20130617_convegno-diocesano-roma.html (accessed August 29, 2016).
2. Pope Francis, 'Message of His Holiness Pope Francis on the Occasion of the 50th Anniversary of the Decree "Apostolicam Acuositatem"' October 22, 2015, quoted in Jack Valero "It's time to consign clericalism to the past, were it belongs," *Crux: Taking the Catholic Pulse*, entry posted June 3, 2016, https://cruxnow.com/global-church/2016/06/03/time-consign-clericalism-past-belongs/ (accessed August 29, 2016).

that the lay apostolate is to evangelize the secular and order the structures of the secular to the highest human and Christian values.[3]

The association of laity and secularity received a deep treatment from Yves Congar, especially in his landmark pre-conciliar text *Lay People in the Church*, and in post-conciliar works such as his 1964 addendums to *Lay People*, his well-known article, 'My Pathfindings in the Theology of the Laity', the books, *Called to Life, I believe in the Holy Spirit*, and the under-studied and as yet untranslated *Un Peuple Messianique*.[4]

The association of laity and secularity, however, has not been without controversy. It has been challenged by theologians such as Peter Coughlan, Bruno Forte, Richard Gaillardetz, and Richard McBrien for ignoring the unity of the Church and for appearing to distance lay people from the center of the church and clergy and religious from engagement with the world.[5]

This paper seeks to identify the ways that and the reasons why Congar associated laity and secularity before and after the Council. While the objections to the association of laity and secularity are not fully engaged, this paper ends by offering some heuristic points for how this association might be better defended theologically should it continue to be maintained.

---

3. *Lumen gentium* 31; *Apostolicam actuositatem* 2; *Gaudium et spes* 43. Vatican II citations are from Austin Flannery, ed, *The Basic Sixteen Documents: Vatican Council II: Constitutions, Decrees, Declarations* (Northport, NY: Costello Publishing, 1996).

4. *Cf Lay People in the Church: A Study for a Theology of Laity*, revised edition, translated by Donald Attwater, (London: Geoffrey Chapman, 1985). French: *Jalons pour une théologie du laïcat*, Unam Sanctam 23 (Paris: Cerf, 1953); 'My Path-Findings in the Theology of Laity and Ministries', in *Jurist* 32 (1972): 169–188; *Called to Life*, translated by William Burridge (New York: Crossroad, 1987); *I Believe in the Holy Spirit*, trans. David Smith, 3 volumes (New York: Crossroad, 1983), *Un Peuple Messianique: L'Église, sacrement du salut: Salut et libération* (Paris: Cerf, 1975.

5. *Cf* Richard P McBrien, 'A Theology of the Laity', in *American Ecclesiastical Review*, 160 (1968): 73–85; Richard R Gaillardetz, 'Shifting Meanings in the Lay-Clergy Distinction', in *Irish Theological Quarterly* 64 (1999): 115–139; Peter Coughlan, *The Search for a Positive Definition or Description of the Laity from Vatican II's Lumen Gentium, 1964, to John Paul II's Christifideles Laici, 1988: A No Through Road* (PhD dissertation, Heythrop College, University of London, 2005); Bruno Forte, *The Church: Icon of the Trinity* (Boston: St Paul Books & Media, 1991), 54–60.

Part One: The First Articulation

It is necessary to begin by establishing what Congar meant by secularity. In Congar's work before the Council his understanding of secularity was articulated in the context of a Church/world/kingdom framework.[6] According to this vision, the secular world stems from the order of creation. The Church stems from the order of redemption. Both are on course for the eschatological kingdom. In between the resurrection and the *Parousia*, the Church has a mission to build itself up internally, to heal the world of the effects of sin and to help order the world to the kingdom. During this time between the first and second comings of Christ, what Congar calls the "entre deux,"[7] the world must be free with respect to the ecclesial order, for God does not wish to force his grace upon it. And so there must be a world distinct from the Church, a world over which the Church does not directly rule, i.e. secularity. In Congar's view, lay Christians exercise their offices of priest, prophet and king both in the world and in the church; but it is with the evangelizing, and ordering of the secular that they are particularly entrusted.

Next, it is necessary to establish how Congar understood the laity. In his early work, Congar often described the Church as composed of structure and life.[8] Structure includes the deposit of faith, the sacraments and the apostolic ministries. Structure comes from above, from the order of redemption. Life is the building of the Church from below. It includes the manifestations of grace in the life of Christians in the world. The *structure* of the Church is a gift which comes from outside the world and which is mediated, in large part, by the clergy. The *life* of the Church is 'the world as believing in Christ'.[9] Thus, in *Lay People*, the laity stand uniquely at the point where Church and world converge. Congar compared the Church, structured this way, to a sacrament, with the structure being the Church's *sacramentum* and its life being the Church's *res*.[10]

---

6. See 'Chapter III: The Position of the Laity: Kingdom, Church and World', in *Laypeople*, 59–107.
7. *Lay People*, 70.
8. See 'Chapter II: Position of a Theology of the Laity', in *Laypeople*, 28–58.
9. Congar, 'The Reasons for Unbelief in our Time', in *Integration* 2/1 (1938): 13–21 and 2/3 (1938): 10–26, at no 3: 21.
10. *Cf Laypeople*, 32 and 57.

It is now possible to describe the several ways Congar associated laity and secularity in the pre-conciliar period. First, he associated them in a way that can be described as existential. Congar contrasts the lay person with the cleric and religious. The religious by virtue of profession and consecration has deliberately removed himself or herself from secularity. The cleric, by ordination, has been firmly identified with the structure of the Church and hence with the order of redemption. Furthermore, the priest's lifestyle removes him from secular work and family life in order that he might be entirely devoted to ecclesial service. Lay people, on the other hand, are not removed from secularity as priests and religious are. Rather, the layperson is located in the secular where he or she accompanies and contributes to the work of the world as it moves in time towards the kingdom.[11] The layperson is the one whose encounter with grace does not remove him from his ordinary place in the world, the world of work and family. The cleric and the religious on the other hand, are characterized by just this existential removal.

Second, Congar claimed a *psychological* association between laity and secularity. Congar argues that the clerical and monastic ways of life come with an occupational hazard,[12] a psychological predisposition of viewing things only in relation to their final end. When this way of viewing things comes to dominate the culture, as it did in the Middle Ages, it leads to the neglect of developing science, art, culture, etc. for their own sake, thus failing to restore creation to its natural integrity, which is integral to the divine plan.[13] The layman, on the other hand, is one for whom 'the substance of things in themselves is real and interesting'.[14] Thus, the psychological association. Incidentally, of Congar's various associations, only the psychological

---

11. Along these lines, Congar wrote in *Lay People*, that the laity 'are called to the same end as clergy or monks . . . but they have to pursue and attain this end without cutting down their involvement in the activities of the world, in the realities of primal creation, in the disappointments, the achievements, the stuff of history . . . Lay people are Christians in the world, there to do God's work *in so far as it must be done in and through the work of the world*' (*Lay People,* 18–19).

12. Religious and priestly life is 'full of dangers' (*Lay People,* 20).

13. *Cf* Ramiro Pellitero, 'Congar's Developing Understanding of the Laity and Their Mission', in *The Thomist* 65 (2001): 327–59, at 336.

14. *Lay People,* 19.

drops out in the post-conciliar period. Congar claimed that it was not explicitly Christian enough.[15]

Thirdly and relatedly, Congar noted a missiological association of laity and secularity. Toward the end of *Lay People*, Congar reflected on New Testament examples of persons who, rather than being called to join Christ's band of wandering followers, were instead allowed to remain in the lay state.[16] Congar argues that these biblical figures are precedents for those called today to the lay vocation, men and women who were not asked to abandon their secular work and familial duties, but rather to seek God in their place and through their ordinary responsibilities.[17] Again, for Congar, as for Rahner,[18] the layperson is the one whose encounter with grace does not remove him from his station. To be sure, Congar was emphatic that the layperson's mission was not exclusively in the world but included as well contribution to the church *ad intra*. But, nonetheless, because the layperson was existentially located in secularity, not removed by special vocation from the world, he or she had a special opportunity and duty to evangelize the secular world and influence the world's temporal structures in a Christian way that was more direct than that of the religious or cleric.

Fourth, Congar made a jurisdictional association between laity and secularity. Congar understood from Christ's rejection of a temporal kingdom that the Church had not been given domain over the temporal world.[19] Congar was anxious that all temptations to medi-

---

15. See his 1964 addendums to *Laypeople*, at page 25 in the Chapman translation.

16. *Cf Laypeople*., 423.

17. 'After having set the faithful apart from the world by his call, God puts them back there and assigns to each a task and duty which also is, in its order, a vocation according to the divine will. God leaves the monk in the world, but here the world is only a setting; he leaves, he sends, the apostle—priest or layperson–in the world, but here the world is only an object on which one works in view of something else; he leaves, or rather he puts, a vast number of men and women in the world, assigning to them the task of co-operating in the work of creation in such a way that it is not alien to their sanctification and salvation, to their co-operation in the kingdom of God', *Lay People*, 423.

18. See Karl Rahner, 'Notes on the Lay Apostolate', in *Theological Investigations*, volume 2, *Man in the Church*, translated Karl H Kruger (Baltimore: Helicon, 1963), 319–352.

19. 'The Church, as a supernatural order of holiness and a divine institution of salvation has no direct responsibility for the world as such' (*Lay People*, 317).

eval integralism be avoided. Only lay Christians, who, though baptized and thus belonging to the kingdom, but were not ordained and thus did not belong in the same way to the institutional structure of the Church, could bear temporal power. He argued that wielding temporal power was the special province of the laity and that 'if they are Christians, they would wield [temporal power] in a Christian way'.[20]

Fifth, Congar associated laity and secularity in a way perhaps best described as ecclesiological. When one considers the Church in its fullness, as both structure and life, *sacrament* and *res*, then one sees that the Church is built from below and not just from above. Being built from below, Church includes the world within it, at least in its life if not in its structure. The laity bring the world into the Church. This is always in a limited way, for there can be no osmosis between Church and world until the eschaton. However, the Church is the 'seed or germ-cell of the kingdom',[21] which will be made up of the world's material, and the layperson might be said to represent the world within the Church before the eschaton.[22]

Having reviewed these five ways Congar associated laity and secularity brings us to the question of why Congar associated laity with secularity? What was at stake here for him?

Congar was motivated by pastoral, humanistic, and missiological concerns. Pastorally, Congar was concerned with identifying the laity positively. Rather than focusing on the laity as 'negative creatures' who do not possess the powers of orders or a special calling to religious life,[23] he suggested the existential and psychological associations. These allowed him to define the laity positively according to their secular character and to celebrate them as such.

Congar's humanistic motivation is manifested in his psychological association and jurisdictional associations. Congar was concerned that the secular truly be embraced and developed according to its own integral nature and he doubted that clerics and religious have

---

20. *Priest and Layman,* translated by PJ Hepburne-Scot (London: Darton, Longmann & Todd, 1967).

21. *Lay People,* 98.

22. *Cf Lay People,* 109–110. One way the lay person brings the world into the Church and represents the world in the Church is through the exercise of the priesthood of the faithful in the context of the liturgy. See 'Chapter IV: The Laity and the Church's Priestly Function', in *Lay People,* 120–233.

23. *Lay People,* 18.

the right mindset for this. Ever wary of Medieval integralism, Congar suggested that the secular is a sphere which belongs to the laity by right and which they should be encouraged to develop.[24]

Finally, Congar detected the urgency of combating secularism and he saw the laity as uniquely positioned to do this. In his missiological association, he explained that the world needs to be evangelized and the entire created realm needs to be healed of sin and prepared for the eschaton through human work. Clergy and religious are not in the world of family and secular work in the same way as laypeople. The task, then, falls in a special way on the laity.[25]

Congar's scheme at the time of *Lay People* follows a rather seamless logic and, thus is easy to understand. There is a world stemming from creation which needs to be healed and ordered to the eschaton. Religious and clergy stand outside and at a distance from the created order, therefore it is integral that the laity embrace this vocation and that the Church affirm it.

Nonetheless, there were some *lacunae* to this scheme. For Congar's critics, it did not say enough about the Church's unity and common mission. It seemed to create rather watertight Church/world compartments. It gave the appearance of either distancing the laity from the center of the Church or clergy and religious from the world. While Congar argued that the formula: 'spiritual things appertain to the priest; temporal things to the layman' was a betrayal of his thought,[26] and went to great lengths in *Lay People* to show how laity were also involved in the Church's life *ad intra*, the links he had made of laity to secularity and clergy to ecclesial ministry were interpreted by many as mutually exclusive.

Part Two: The Second Articulation

In his post-conciliar work, Congar's ecclesiology developed in some significant ways. In considering the Church world relationship, for example, Congar admitted that the lines between Church and world

---

24. *Cf Lay People*, 20–24. See also Congar, 'Respect for the Apostolate of the Laity among Priests and Religious', in *Christians Active in the World*, translated by PJ Hepburne Scott (New York: Herder and Herder, 1968), 3–23.
25. On this point, see especially Congar's article 'Reasons for Unbelief in our Time'.
26. *Lay People*, 24.

were more permeable than he had stated before. This permeability is due to such things as the intrinsic openness of nature to grace, the workings of grace outside the visible boundaries of the Church, and the re-centering of our image of the Church on the people of God who are engaged in the world rather than exclusively on the hierarchy set apart from the world.[27]

There were also changes in the way Congar envisaged the structure of the Church. Following Schillebeeckx, Congar recognized a conciliar ecclesiological de-centralization away from a papal and priestly ecclesial center toward a re-centering of ecclesial imagery in the whole people of God. Accordingly, in his own ecclesiology there was new focus on the essential unity of the Church and on the presence of a multiplicity of charisms and ministries within an ecclesial community considered first according to unity.[28]

Thus, central to Congar's post-conciliar ecclsiology is pneumatology. The Holy Spirit builds up the Church both charismatically and sacramentally. The Spirit works on the whole Church, fostering, at once, both unity and diversity, commissioning the members of the Church for their work, primarily through the sacraments, and strengthening them for their particular duties with charisms and graces.[29] Significantly, Congar no longer omitted the laity from the structure of the Church. The structure of the Church comes from the sacraments of baptism, confirmation, and orders. The whole Church is then together *sacramentum* to the world.[30]

Although Congar placed greater emphasis on antecedent unity in his later ecclesiology, he was concerned about preserving a sense of distinctions. As early as 1964, Congar cautioned that post-conciliar ecclesiology might end up collapsing the Church into an undifferentiated body.[31] He noted that the main Vatican II images of Church implied both unity and distinction. The body of Christ has many parts and many members. The Church as sacrament is made by the

---

27. See especially Congar's 'The Role of the Church in the Modern World', in *Commentary on the Documents of Vatican II* Volume 5, edited by Herbert Vogrimler and others, translated by WJ O'Hara (New York: Herder and Herder, 1969), 202–223.
28. *Cf Called to Life*, 21; 'My Path-findings', 175–178.
29. *Cf I Believe in the Holy Spirit* 2:5–64.
30. *Cf I Believe in the Holy Spirit* 3:271.
31. *Cf Lay People*, 25.

various sacraments (Baptism, confirmation, Eucharist, orders, matrimony) which also differentiate vocationally. Even people of God, if understood in reference to its Old Testament roots, admitted of different groups, different vocations: the Levites for example, and the prophets.[32]

While Congar thought it was completely legitimate to identify lay Christians simply as Christian faithful, as *Christifideles sine additio*, he noted that this did not say enough about their specificity. He argued that a full appreciation of the laity unfolded only by way of contrast with the existential conditions of clerics and religious and that this contrast would always lead back to the topic of laity and secularity. While the cleric and religious also exist and mission in the created world, these vocations entailed some kind of consecration and removal from ordinary life that differentiates their existential condition from that of lay Christians. If the first articulation stated these differences absolutely, Congar now stated them with more qualifications, but he still stated them, because he thought they remained true.[33]

Before the Council, the association of laity and secularity was linked to strong dichotomies between the center and periphery, structure and life, and the above and below of the Church. After Vatican II, Congar emphasized more the antecedent unity of the Church and the particular symbolization or signification of the different vocations within that antecedent and over-arching unity. For example, both priest and lay person are firmly situated in the people of God, and both are recognised as contributing to building up of the body through ministries and services. However, the priest continues to represent to the Church Christ as he stands over and against the body, and to the world the Church as a divine society set apart. The lay person continues to represent to the Church the worldly element which is inherent to the Church's sacramentality, and to the world the way in which the Church is embedded within secularity as leaven. These symbolisations, however, are not arbitrary. They depend on sacraments, charisms, callings and graces which condition one's existence.[34]

---

32. *Cf Called to Life*, 68; *Un Peuple Messianique*, 81; *IBHS* 2:11; 'The Church: The People of God', translated by Kathryn Sullivan, *Concilium*, 1 (1965): 7–19

33. See Congar, 'Laïc et laïcat' in *Dictionnaire de spiritualité*, Volume 9 (Paris: Beacuchesne, 1976), cols. 79–108; 'The Laity' in *Vatican II: An Interfaith Appraisal*, edited by John H Miller (Notre Dame, IN: University of Notre Dame Press, 1966), 239–249.

34. *Cf* 'My Path-Findings', 174–178; *Un Peuple MEssianique*, 173.

Finally, in *Un Peuple Messianique*, Congar argued that some sense of dualism must be maintained both between the Church and the world and between the cleric and the layperson.[35] The Church, he explained, exists in a tension, the classic both-and of in the world yet not of the world. The Church must be understood as something different from the world, even in its solidarity and dialogue with the world. For Congar, clerics and religious particularly represent and carry the Church as something different from the world, a divine society set apart from the world. They remind us of that aspect of what the Church is. And this is appropriate to them since their vocations have called them to be uprooted from ordinary secular work and family. However, because they are existentially set apart they do not have the same opportunity to evangelize the secular; and because they represent the Church as a divine society of positive law, they cannot govern the secular. Laypeople are more associated with the Church, not as it appears as a society set apart, but as the people of God, that is, the Church emerging from, standing with and in the world, evangelizing and ordering that world while being in deep solidarity with it. They are ideally positioned to evangelize and order the world. Furthermore, they are free—because they do not represent the Church as divine society of positive law—to take political charge of the secular. All are part of the same church, but the existential locations, ecclesiological representations, and particular missions remain different. So, we see that Congar's humanistic and missiological motivations are still present, driving his insistence that laity and secularity must be linked.

Part Three: Conclusion

While Congar maintained the association of laity and secularity throughout his career, it is disputable whether he provided a satisfying enough theological justification for it that also sufficiently qualified it. For Jacques Servais and Anthony Oelrich, Congar's work, even after the Council, remains overly dependent on unresolved schematic dualisms.[36] Congar is content to say that on the one hand, the Church

---

35. For what follows, see *Un Peuple Messianique*, 172–177.
36. See Jacques Servais, 'Le statut théologique du laïc en debat: Yves Congar et Hans Urs von Balthasar', in *Chrétiens dans la société actuelle: L'apport de Hans Urs von*

is this (for example, the people of God), and on the other hand, the Church is that (for example, the divine society of positive law). On the one hand, the lay people are fully engaged *ad intra*, and, on the other hand, the lay person is especially to be involved in the church's mission *ad extra* and so forth, without bringing into higher relief the theological coherence behind his many both-ands.

Congar's framework could be made more defensible in a couple of ways. First, suggests Servais, Congar's association would benefit from a more explicit account of analogy. What is predicated principally to one vocation might be participated in by the others either vicariously or even directly but in a different degree than the *analogatum princeps* is. So, for example, we can say that the laity have a special call to work in the secular; the clergy a special call to build up the body from within, and the religious a special call to signify eschatology and radical discipleship—but none of these predications omit the participation of the others in what is the primary call of another. The underlying theological principles behind such an approach are the analogy of being whereby what is predicated principally to God is participated in a secondary way by his creation, and also, the notion of Trinitarian appropriation whereby what is appropriated work or mission of one person of the Trinity is nonetheless participated in by all three persons, for example, the Father as creator, the Son as redeemer, and the Holy Spirit as sanctifier. Following this line, we can agree with Pope Paul VI that the entire Church has a 'secular dimension', but also see that the laity bear particular responsibility for it.[37] It is appropriated to them.

Second, in order to better secure that the lay-secular association does not distance laity from the center of the Church, Hans Urs von Balthasar's recognition that at every level the Church is as an event of communion between God and the world in a helpful insight.[38] For

---

Balthasar, edited by Didier Gonneaud and Philippe Charpentier de Beauvillé (Soceval: Magny-les-Hammeaux, France, 2006), 131–158; Anthony Oelrich, *A Church Fully Engaged: Yves Congar's Vision of Ecclesial Authority* (Collegeville, MN: Liturgical Press, 2011), 121–123.

37. Paul VI, 'Talk to the Members of Secular Institutes', 2 February1972: *AAS* 64 (1972), 208, quoted in John Paul II, Post-Synodal Apostolic Exhortation *Christifideles Laici*, no 15, in John Paul II, *Apostolic Exhortations* (Tervandrum: Carmel International Publishing House, 2005).

38. See Hans Urs von Balthasar, 'The Layman and the Church', in *The Spouse of the Word*, Volume 2 of *Explorations in Theology*, 315–331. (San Francisco: Ignatius Press, 1991).

Balthasar, the first level of the Church is Christ and he has a human
nature, thus a Marian/worldly/lay contribution to the very hypostatic
union. The second level of the Church is the Eucharist, what *Sacro-
sanctum concilium* calls the 'principal manifestation of the Church'.
Here, God becomes one with his people in a liturgical event of communion. The world is represented in the Eucharist by the people and
their gifts. The third level of the Church is the culture when the people
bring grace and gospel to bear on the structures of the world in ordinary life. This too is a level of Church says Balthasar because Church
is found wherever nature and grace converge. This view helps to show
that being lay and secular in no way distances one from the center of
the Church, for every level of the Church is in fact an event of communion between God and world and thus there is always a lay and
worldly element within the Church wherever she is found. In some
ways, Congar gets close to saying this in his description of Church as
sacrament in *Un Peuple Messianique*,[39] and even in his pre-conciliar
descriptions of the Church being built from both above and below,
but it remains a somewhat incipient insight for Congar and, arguably
is never fully integrated into his association of laity and secularity.

In sum, while capable of further development in some areas, Congar's articulation of the association of laity and secularity is a significant contribution to contemporary ecclesiology. Congar helps show
why, in the words of John Paul II, 'the lay faithful's position in the
Church . . . comes to be fundamentally defined by their *newness in
Christian life* and distinguished by their *secular character*.'[40]

---

39. Congar's view in *Un Peuple Messianique* can be stated thusly: First, after the
pattern of Christ, the Church as sacrament depends on the presence or inclusion
of the world for its visible material aspect (13–14, 24). Second, liturgy is where the
Church becomes sacrament, 'human and divine, visible and rich with invisible
realities' (13). Third, the world itself has an orientation to becoming Church in
the Eucharist. While ultimately Church and world converge perfectly only in
the eschaton, they do so in an anticipatory way now in the Mass (144, 159–160).
Fourth, laypeople are existentially located in the secular where they exercise their
common baptismal priesthood. While it is true that their consecration of the
world does not subsume it into the Church, their priestly offerings reach a pre-
eschatological fulfillment when they unite their self-offering to Christ's within
through the ministry of ordained priests in the context of the celebration of the
Eucharist (159–60; see also 'The Laity', 244).
40. *Christifideles laici*, no 15.

Meeting Yves Congar

Thomas Franklin O'Meara, OP

The French Dominicans—so important in the life of the Catholic Church in the twentieth century—made contributions to areas of church life ranging from ecumenism to church art. One of them, Yves Congar, wrote of the excitement of the years after World War II leading to the Ecumenical Council Vatican II. 'Anyone who did not live during the years of French Catholicism after the war missed one of the finest movements in the life of the church. Through a slow emergence from misery, one tried in the great freedom of a fidelity as profound as life, to rejoin in a Gospel way the world, a world of which the church could become an integral part for the first time in centuries.'[1] Congar joined research in the history of church forms to an advocacy of the movement for Christian unity. Richard McBrien wrote of him: 'By any reasonable account, Yves Congar is the most distinguished ecclesiologist of this century and perhaps of the entire post-Tridentine era. No modern theologian's spirit was accorded fuller play in the documents of Vatican II than Congar's.'[2] The following pages record a few personal meetings with Père Congar.

A Dominican Master General in Iowa

In September of 1953 I was a freshman at Loras College in Dubuque, Iowa. I had expressed interest in becoming a Dominican priest. The Dominicans required two years of college before they admitted men

---

1. Congar, Dialogue between Christians (London: Chapman, 1966), 32.
2. McBrien, 'Church and Ministry. The Achievement of Yves Congar', *Theology Digest,* 32 (1985): 203.

to the Order through entrance into the novitiate. About twenty fresh-
men and sophomores lived in a small dormitory, Smyth Hall under
the pre-novitiate direction of two priests who taught theology and
history at the College.

During that autumn, Emmanuel Suarez, OP, Master General of
the Dominicans, came to Dubuque. He was a Spaniard and an expert
in church law. The Dominicans had their seminary, their *studium*,
a theological school, in Dubuque. After Suarez visited the friars at
St Rose Priory, the *studium*, he came to Loras. We met him and had
our picture taken with him (someone sent me a copy of the picture
around 2005).

About a month later in October of 1953, Cardinal Pizzardo, director of the Holy Office in Rome at the Vatican (formerly 'The Supreme
Sacred Congregation of the Roman and Universal Inquisition'), wrote
to the head of the Dominicans, Fr Suarez: 'You know well the new
ideas and tendencies, not only exaggerated but even erroneous, that
are developing in the realms of theology, canon law, and society, ideas
finding a considerable resonance in certain religious orders . . . so-
called theologians 'with brilliant phrases and generalizations' teach
falsehood.'[3] At this time, in April, 1952, Congar wrote in his journal
'The Pope [Pius XII] is influenced by his entourage . . . by Cardinal Pizzardo, whose influence is considerable at the present time . . .
Cardinal Pizzardo is a complete nullity; in Rome everyone laughs at
him, but he is a perfect domestic servant.'[4] The hostility of some in
the central administration of the church had been increasing in the
decades after World War II as the French Church strove to renew its
life and appeal to people. Vatican offices threatened to curtain the
Dominicans, and to appease the Vatican, Suarez flew in February,
1954, to Paris. He removed from office the three French provincials
and the provincial directors of studies. Some well-known professors
of theology were forbidden to teach or publish. This unprecedented
move went against the democratic structure of the Order of Preachers: Congar said it was 'unheard of'. In Paris, the newspaper *Le Monde*
called it 'a raid on the Dominicans'.[5]

3. Cited in François Leprieur, *Quand Rome condamne* (Paris: Cerf, 1989), 42–45.
4. Congar, *Journal of a Theologian, 1946–1956* (Adelaide: ATF Theology, 2015), 260.
5. See Thomas O'Meara, 'Raid on the Dominicans: The Repression of 1954', *America*,
    170 (1994): 8–16; Johannes Bunnenberg, 'In den Fängen des Hl. Offiziums. "Die
    düsteren Jahre" des Dominikaners Yves Congar', *Wort und Antwort*, 44 (2003):
    19–24.

The French friars recognised that their leader's measures were aimed at preserving their existence, and they submitted if some protested. Congar spoke sharply about the contrast between new directions in theology, religious education and liturgy and the metaphysical rules of the Baroque and the late nineteenth century. He submitted and awaited better times. He wrote to his mother at that time: 'What I am blamed for is usually very little. Most of the time, whatever problem is raised about an idea in my work is explained in the following line in that same work. What has put me in the wrong (in their eyes) is not having said false things but having said things they do not want to be said.'[6]

Six months later, in June of 1954 while driving north from Rome, Suarez and his Dominican secretary were killed in a car accident.

Those tumultuous events for the French Dominicans occurred in the months just after Suarez came to Loras College.

Congar in Rome. An Adviser at Vatican II

Movements for reformation had been brewing in Northern Europe among theologians and charismatic leaders in most of the twentieth century. In the 1950s they reached a climax. 'Do not extinguish the Spirit', Paul wrote to the Thessalonians, and Karl Rahner quoted those words in a first essay on the possibilities of the Ecumenical Council just called by Pope John XXIII. For that assembly the Holy Spirit had prepared an extraordinary number of men and women from around the world who contributed new and old ideas. Congar's writings including translations of them into various languages are estimated at 1700. In one year, 1937, he published the book *True and False Reform* and fourteen articles: on the theology of mysticism, Catholicism and Protestantism, Thomas Aquinas and truth, the spiritual writer from the Baroque Louis Chardon, Christendom and France, and on ecumenical conferences.

In 1960, Pope John XXIII named Congar a consulter for the coming ecumenical council, Vatican II. His creativity, evident by the time he was thirty, was active in the agenda and the event of Vatican II. The Dominican theologian and biographer of Congar Jean-Pierre

---

6. Étienne Fouilloux, 'Lettre du Père Congar à sa mère', *La Vie Spirituelle*, 154 (2000):137.

Jossua describes him as 'a figure emblematic of the theology of the Council, perhaps the most known theologian of the century', while a recent European ecclesiologist Hervé Legrand observes, 'It is very rare that the personal destiny of a theologian prefigures and influence the course of the life of the Church'.[7]

During the years when I was a student in Germany after 1963, I would go down to Rome from Munich, accompanying family and friends visiting from the United States. During the fall sessions of Vatican II in the evenings you could attend lectures being given to groups of bishops by the theologians, 'the experts' of the Council. One night I was sitting along the Tiber in the conciliar autumn after hearing Congar give a talk to bishops from Latin American countries. It had been a talk to bishops about bishops. He stressed the bishop in the first centuries of the church as the leader of a particular, local church. He firmly set aside the ecclesiology of the bishop as a vicar, an ambassador, a branch manager for the Pope. The Pope was himself one bishop.

One day in 1964 I had just said goodbye to relatives among the splendors of Rome. Tomorrow I would take the long train trip—twelve hours—back to Munich. I was visiting on the street with a Dominican from my Province, a friend who was doing a doctorate in canon law in Rome. A long black automobile pulled up next to us the street. With difficulty Yves Congar got out. He gave my Dominican friend, Bert, a stack of mimeographed dossiers. Bert was a theological adviser to the bishops of Nigeria; for some years, he had lived and worked in Nigeria at Dominican parishes and schools there. 'For the bishops of Nigeria—and right away!' Congar said. He then got back into the car with difficulty, and they drove away. The bishops of Belgium had found rooms for Congar at some Belgian institute, and because the Dominican was increasingly hindered by a neurological disease, they found a car and a driver for him. The Italian and Spanish friars in Rome with whom he at first lodged largely ignored him.

Congar was always in a hurry, writing and then distributing the pages of commentaries on the drafts of the Council's texts. Those pages critiquing the many drafts of the Council's documents, he said, 'were as numerous as the leaves falling from the autumn trees in Rome'. Later I read that, the theologian, hurrying and looking ahead,

---

7.   MM Wolff, *Gott und Mensch. Ein Beitrag Yves Congars zum ökumenischen Dialog* (Frankfurt: Knecht, 1990), 13.

would urge his driver to go through red lights if they did not see any cars coming on the cross street. 'V*ite, vite.*' The work of the Council pressed upon him.

The Council came to an end in the first week of December of its fourth session. In his diary Congar wrote for December 7, 1965, that at the end when the bishops voted on the conciliar texts, 'I left slowly and with difficulty, barely able to stand. A great many bishops congratulated me, thanked me. To a good extent, it was my work, they said. Looking at things objectively, I did a great deal to prepare for the Council, elaborating and diffusing the ideas the Council consecrated. At the Council itself, I did a great deal of work. Thus what was read out this morning came, to a very large extent, from me.'[8] Theologians and bishops recognised how important, how unique he was. 'Congar belongs to those theologians whose work has so entered into the theology of Vatican II that the Council's historical origin is found in his power and originality . . . Congar is personally co-responsible for the history of Catholic theology in recent times.'[9]

At the end of the second session of the Council, Pope Paul VI had a reception for the theologians who had worked so hard. Because of his neurological disease Congar attended in a wheelchair. The pope gave to each of the theologians a beautiful book from the Vatican publishing house. Two years later, at the end of the fourth session, he held a second reception of gratitude. Again he gave each a book. When he came to Congar, the Dominican said: 'But, Holy Father, you already gave me this book.' The startled Pope said he would find a different book.

Congar was an honest person, a tough person. He said that the Gestapo, the KGB, and the Vatican's Holy Office had the same mentality. 'I ought to know. I dealings with two of them.'

A letter from Yves Congar

In the years right after Vatican II there was a move in the United States towards restoring a new (but quite venerable and traditional) church form, the council. Parish councils were set up, and often diocesan councils. Offering some balance to an ecclesiastical autocrat—from parish

---

8.   Congar, *My Journal of the Council*, 870–1
9.

pastor to pope—seemed worthwhile. Should there be a church council on the national level? For the United States? A step towards this was taken for America in 1969 with the establishment of a national advisory council composed of bishops and non-bishops to exercise oversight over central church initiatives. One of the advisory council's first suggestions was to produce a feasibility study of a national pastoral council. This had its climax in a conference held at Mundelein College, Chicago, in August,1970; 101 dioceses and thirty-six national organizations were represented. I was invited to be present at this meeting by some group. It was suggested to those coming as theological advisers that they should contact other theologians for their views. I wrote to Yves Congar, asking what he thought of a national pastoral council. He answered with a short, dense letter, written in English.

He did not really address the nature and value of a pastoral council on a national level but touched on the nature and value of serious institutional change, and new institutions in the church after Vatican II. He began: 'It is astonishing how the post-Council has so little to do with the Council.'[10] He drew this into the ambiguous guidance of the Pope. 'There lies, I think, the tragedy of Pope Paul's Pontificate because nobody is so faithful to the Council as he is. But the post-conciliar questions are new and radical.' Then he contrasted the *aggiornamento* of before and during the Council with the new questions already multiplying, only a few years later. *Aggiornamento* 'means changes and adaptations to a new situation, assuming the principles of the original institution. It is not a new creation, though new creations can, and even must, be done in the Church . . .' He implies that the present time is not calling for more 'updating' but for some really new directions and organizations in the church.

The advisory council reported to the bishops the following year. A national pastoral council was desirable but not immediately feasible—more preparation was needed before going ahead. In January, 1973, however, the Vatican's Congregation for the Clergy sent the world's bishops a letter saying national pastoral councils were not opportune. Not a few thought that the letter was partly in response to the feasibility study in the United States.[11]

---

10. Congar, Letter to Thomas O'Meara (Sept. 12, 1970), Couvent d'Études des Frères Prêcheurs Le Saulchoir, Étiolles, 91, Soisy-sur-Seine, France.

11. See 'The National Pastoral Council of a Christian Church: Ecclesiastical Accessory or Communal Voice?' in *A National Pastoral Council: Pro and Con* (Washington, DC: USCC, 1971), 21–34.

Journal Entry for January 7, 1974, Paris, en route to Nigeria.

In 1974, I stopped in Paris on my way to teach for a semester in Nigeria. At the Dominican priory of St Jacques I had a brief visit with Congar and wrote in a journal. 'Père Congar. He looks old, tired, unexcited, as I enter, sitting behind a large desk. He extends his left hand because his right is lame. The desk is crowded with papers— many *'petites choses,'* he says. He repeats his reasons for not accepting the request of the Dominicans in the Midwest to come to the United States for a lecture tour. We thought the trip would offer appreciation, leisure, and new fields to explore. At present, he says, there are too many demands especially now at the time of the seven hundred anniversary of the death of Thomas Aquinas.'[12]

I mention that I am working on German thought in the nineteenth century. I remark how Hegel for much of the twentieth century was seen as an oddity, someone bizarre and erroneous. Congar observes, *'il est devenu un Père de l'Église'* ('Now he has become a 'Father of the Church').

When Congar smiles and relaxes he becomes younger: his blue eyes are especially prominent, dominating the Gallic, Celtic face. He is sad about the future of his Province: he speaks of a 'professional' (for example, like an engineer) employment of the young. I think that he misunderstands this and is too much weighed down by it. When I mention, 'Munich,' he says, 'Grabmann', alluding to the great German pioneer of medieval studies and the institute named after him in Bavaria. He refers to the Curia in Rome as being 'a non-being' (*'la néant de la Curie'*). The view that the bishop is an ambassador of the pope is *'stupide, presque héréticale'* ('stupid, almost heretical').

That morning, after I saw Congar, I visited at the Sorbonne an exhibit on its history with a number of documents. Among them was one from Pope Gregory XII establishing the university. And too, a letter from Pope Honorius III mentions that the Dominicans would soon arrive.

Denouement

Congar in the years around the Council pointed out that the challenge posed by the modern person and society was twofold: the perspec-

---

12. A decade later Congar wrote to American Dominicans on the occasion of other invitations: 'Letter from Yves Congar, O.P., *Theology Digest*, 32:3 (1985): 213.

tive and creativity of the subject, and the unfolding of history. The re-acceptance of history by the church is central. The church really, realistically, lives in history: it cannot avoid time with its expansions and its delays. 'It is not *in spite* of time and its course but in them that the Church brings forth the gifts of God and realizes them.'[13] He often said that what was decisive about the Council was that it had re-entered history. So not only charismatic laity and educated theologians but also bishops were speaking of things new and hope-filled and were listening to the Holy Spirit. The historian of theologies saw the Council as a beginning, and he expected further developments and deeper reforms to occur. The upheavals that arrived in the postconciliar era were long overdue, he observed, and their roots lay not in Vatican II but in the constrictive decades (even centuries) before it.

His neurological illness had made his work in Rome difficult, and by the late 1960s he was often in a wheelchair. In 1984, he moved from the Priory of Saint-Jacques to the military hospital of Les Invalides, a hospital for veterans, indeed, founded by Napoleon; it was the first hospital for veterans. As World War II began, in 1939 Congar was drafted into the army (priests and religious were not exempt) and was captured early on. Over the following years he made five attempts to escape; he ends up in harsher camps and eventually at the famous maximum security prison of Colditz. One thing caused by the war most upset him: the loss of time from research and work. But, as he noted, he did learn German well.

John Paul II honored Congar at the very end of his life, creating him a cardinal. The ceremony was in the Baroque chapel of the military hospital. Dignitaries of the church from Rome and Paris attended; sacristans and acolytes moved around cardinals and bishops. When Père Congar arrived he was accompanied by two soldiers, in fatigues and boots. Some dignitaries in crimson capes were shocked. As he explained, the veterans' hospital was now his community, his local church, and he wanted his present-day community to take part in what was given to him, a member. Good ecclesiology to the end.

---

13. 'Pour un sens vrai de l'Église', *Cette Église que j'aime* (Paris: Cerf, 1968), 94. 'The vision of the Council—that of *Lumen Gentium*—has been resolutely that of history of salvation, given a destiny by eschatology' (Congar, 'Situation ecclésiologique au moment de 'Ecclesiam Suam' et passage à une église dans l'itinéraire des hommes', René Rémond, ed, *Le Concile de Vatican II. Son Église. Peuple de Dieu et corps du Christ* (Paris: Beauchesne, 1984), 27.

He was unable to experience directly or fully the renewal of ministry and church around the world as his theological principles remained influential. He died on June 22, 1991. At Congar's funeral, three spoke: Cardinal Lustiger, Archbishop of Paris; Timothy Radcliffe, OP, Master of the Dominican Order; and a general from the French army.

How strange. Someone in the vows of religious life, under the constraints of the late-Baroque papacy, an unappreciated pioneer, a constant worker—and yet in its obituary a Paris newspaper called Yves Congar 'a free man'.[14]

---

14. *La Vie* (Nov. 10, 1994): 8

InterfaceTheology 3/1 2017

Sermon for the Funeral of our brother Cardinal Yves Congar OP

Timothy Radcliffe OP

Today we have come together to give thanks to God for our brother Yves Congar, and to pray for him. We give thanks by celebrating the sacrament of gratitude, the eucharist.. I was priveleged to celebrate this sacrament with fr.Yves almost every day during my year at St.Jacques, and it remains for us the sacrament of communion, in which we are one with the living and the dead.

We give thanks not only for our brother Yves, but with him. Today we share in his gratitude for all that he received and was. He used to say that there were "trois grâces de son existence", the friendships that he made in the prisons of Colditz and Lubeck during the war; his membership of the Dominican Order, and the Second Vatican Council. I would suggest that each of these moments of grace were moments of suffering, but suffering transformed into community. It was a theme perhaps prefigured in the card he had printed for his first Mass, which showed St.Dominic at the foot of the cross, and which has a quotation from the English poet, Tennyson, "But none of the ransomed ever knew how deep were the waters crossed". Certainly at the beginning of his life our brother could never have imagined how deep would be the waters he would h ave to cross in his life as a brother, a theologian and a man.

Let us look at each of these moments, and give thanks together with our brother for them.

When fr.Yves was first imprisoned during the war, near Berlin, he gave lectures and preached on liberty and against nazism, in explicit disobedience to his captors. This says much about him. He was first and foremost a teacher, in whatever circumstances. And he was a courageous teacher, teaching what might endanger his life. Because he refused to stop teaching, he was punished by being sent to the terrible prisons of Colditz and then Lubeck. He said that here the most important thing that he learnt was how to cook noodles. In prison, you had to learn how to survive and how to help each other. Here, in this place of deprivation he learnt the great richness of friendship, and he made friends whom he kept until he died.

The second of the graces of his life was his membership of the Dominican Order. He received the habit in 1925 at Amiens, and started his studies at the convent of Le Saulchoir near Tornai. Le Saulchoir evokes for us not just a place but an intellectual community, above all of Congar, Chenu and Ferret. They formed a school of theology. It was characteristic of fr.Yves that his theological work was not that of a solitary scholar, but as a member of an intellectual community, in which you learn to give and to receive. One of the great sufferings of his life was when this very community became the focus of suspicion by the Roman curia. He learnt of the condemnation of Chenu's book, *le Saulchoir, une ecole de theologie*, while he was still in prison in Germany. It was the beginning of a time of suffering of which I shall say more in a moment.

But for fr.Yves entering the Order was a grace not just because he found an intellectual community but because he found friendship and ultimately love. This became more and more apparent as he became increasingly immobile due to his neurological illness. He had felt the first symtpoms in 1936. So two thirds of his life were marked by this ever deeper entry in a physical suffering, which must have been spiritually hard to endure. It was a suffering that he regarded as a source of much of his work as a theologian: it was the chalice of Jesus that he drank. He said towardsd the end of his life, 'en m'unissant à ce calice, je peux encore apporter quelque chose"

What he above all learnt from this suffering was communion and friendship with his brothers in St.Dominic. He said "J'ai surtout compris depuis ma maladie, et ayant tourjours besoin du service de mes frères, . . . que ce que nous pouvons raconter et dire, aussi sublime soit-il, ne vaut pas cher is cela n'est pas accompagné d'une praxis, d'une action réelle, concrète, de service, d'amour. Je pense que j'ai un peu manqué a cela dans ma vie, j'ai été un peu trop intellectuel". So once again we find suffering which is transformed into communion, into love.

What he discovered as a theologian and as a broither, in his intellectual work and in his suffering, was how we have need of our brothers. As God says to St.Catherine of Siena "I could well have made human beings in such a way that they all had everything, but I prefered to give different gifts to different people, so that they would all need each other."

His particular service of the brothers, his *diakonia*, was hard intellectual work. And he certainly worked, incessantly writing. I remember, when I was a student at the convent of St.Jacques, that he could be seen every morning at his desk, in the room opening onto to the garden, at work from seven in the morning until ten at night. It was the hard labour of his service of the truth. He wrote, "Le vrai, j'y ai consacré ma vie . . . c'est vraiment la dame de ma vie. J'ai d'ailleurs souvent écrit cela en tête de mes textes: 'Veritas domina mea' "But the truth that he served was not an abstract truth, but the truth of the gospel as disclosed in the dynamism of history, the lived truth, made real in the lives of men and women. He even once quoted the famous words of Peguy "Non pas le vrai, mais le réel." "c'est à dire le vrai avec l'historicité, avec son état concret dans le devinir, dans le temps." It is through this lived history that we enter into the eternity of God.

One of my most powerful memories of fr.Yves was of the time we toured the caethdral of Chartres, with me pushing his wheelchair, while he explained the theology of the stained glass, the true made real in colour and light, incarnate in the beauty of art.

Third and perhaps the greatest grace for which fr.Yves gave thanks was the Council. And it is here, above all, where we can see the mystery of suffering transformed into communion. From the beginning of his intellectual work, fr.Yves struggled with the themes that were to be central to the Council, the role of the laity, christian unity, the reform of the Church. In 1950 appeared *Vraie et Fauuse reforme dans l'Eglise,* and in 1953 *Jalons pour une theologie du laicat.* All of his work was marked by a deep love of the Church, a love without reservation. He wrote to me, after he was elevated to the cardinalate, that "l'Eglise et son mystere a ete et demeurele tout de ma vie de chretien et de theologien". But was precisely this love that led him to struggle for a Church that was liberated from too narrow and juridical identity, that was a people on pilgrimage towards the perfect communion of the Kingdom.

All this labour of love brought, at first, only suspicion and condemnation from Rome. He was silenced, forbidden to teach and sent into exile in 1954. Four months in Jerusalem, then toRome, and a year in Cambridge, where the brethren have a clear memory of him practicing his yoga exercises by hanging upside down in the trees in the garden. Then he moved to Strasbourg. He bore this experience with typical courage and with hope. He was enough of an historian to know that the Church arrives at new insights often after great resistence, and he was enough of a christian to believe that the Spirit eventually leads the community to truth. All he said was this:" Ma resistance ne peut consister qu'en ceci, ne jamais lacher mon service de la Verite'

Typically he found that this suffering bore fruit. In exile in Jerusalem, he was bowled over by the beauty of the remains of the Temple, and a sense of God's dwelling with humanioty throughout all its history of suffering and exile.

And the fruit of all this suffering was that deep transformation of the Church which was the Second Vatican Council. The suffering of exile led to the renewal of that community of the Church for which he gave his life, "cette Eglise que j'aime" "Eglise de dieu, ma mere". The Council was an **experience** of communion, of what the Church is called to be, a Church of dialogue, led by the Spirit, not turned in upon itself but open to the world and its sufferings," vaste monde, ma paroisse".

fr.Yves was deeply and rightly proud of his contribution to the documents of the Council, especially to *Lumen Gentium*. But it was a good and humble pride, like that of a craftsman who likes to show you his work. His only sorrow was that sometimes the Church seems to have returned to a narrower and more rigid existence.

So these are the three moments of grace for which fr.Yves gave thanks in his life.. But there is a fourth for which he longed and laboured and which is yet to be given, and that was the unity of all christians. In 1930, he had meditated on that great text of St.John's gospel, the prayer of Jesus that we may all be one, *ut sint unum*. From then onwards he felt a deep personal mission to work for the healing of the divisions of Christianity. In fact one might say that *all* of Congar's theology was ecumenical. The question to which he always returned, was "quelles diversités sont possibles dans la communion?"

The disunity of christians is, of course, a great wound in the witness of Christianity, and fr.Yves seemed even to associate his own personal suffering and illness with the cause of unity. He first noticed that he was ill while he was giving the series of conferences on christian unity that were to become his famous book, *Chretiens desunis*, during the week of christian unity in 1936. "Mes conferences duraient une heure et, dès ce moment-là, j'avais un premier signe de la maladie: je me rapppelle très bien que je m'appuyais du bras droit sur le bord de la chaire." Perhaps his hope was that this drinking of the cup of suffering could be healing for the churches.

He understood that the healing of these divisions demanded not only an understanding of the views of the others, but a deeper communion, a communion of love, a sympathy of spirit. He kept an orthodoxy icon from St.Petersberg in his room. As Jean Pierre Josshua wrote, "il comprenait qu'il fallait d'abord *aimer* ce type de croyants qu'ont ete les premiers reformateurs, les saints et theologiens orthodoxes, afin de les comprendre, quitte a ne pas s'accorder avec eux."

The fourth grace would have been for fr.Yves to have seen the healing of these divisions, the restoration of communion. Let us pray that in Christ now he rejoices in the love that heals all wounds, and is the perfection of all communion. And let us be one with him now in the celebration of this eucharist, the sacrament of suffering transformed into perfect unity.

List of Contributors

Eric T de Clermont-Tonnerre OP, is a Dominican Friar of the Province of France, was Provincial of the Province from 1992 till 2001, from 2005 until 2013 he was Director of Éditiones du Cerf, Paris.

Jannette Gary, RSM, was Faculty member at Jesuit Theological College, Melbourne, 2004–2014, and Principal of the College, 2012–2014, and after this taught in a number of theological colleges within the University of Divinity, Melbourne. She died in December 2017.

Stefan Gigacz, has recently completed a PhD on Joseph Cardjin at the Second Vatican Council and lives in Perth, Australia.

Thomas Franklin O'Meara OP, is a Dominican Friar of the Central Province of the Dominican Friar in the USA and Emeritus Warren Professor of Theology, University of Notre Dame, Indiana, USA.

Christian Raab OSB, is a Benedictine at Saint Meinrad's Archabbey in Indianna, USA and Assistant Professor of Systematic Theology at Saint Meinrad Seminary and School of Theology, Saint Meinrad, Indiana, USA.

Timothy Radcliffe OP, is a Dominican Friar of the English Province, and former Master of the Order of Preachers, the Dominicans, from 1992 to 2001.